LEADERSHIP ON THE OTHERSIDE

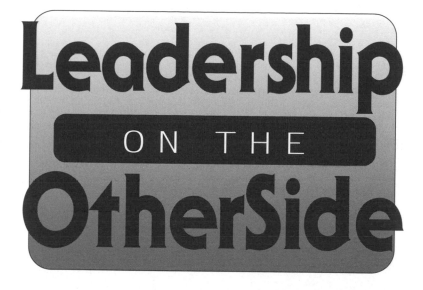

Leadership ON THE OtherSide

No Rules, Just Clues

Bill Easum

ABINGDON PRESS/Nashville

LEADERSHIP ON THE OTHERSIDE
No Rules, Just Clues

Copyright © 2000 by Abingdon Press

This book is printed on recycled, acid-free, elemental-chlorine–free paper.

Library of Congress Cataloging-in-Publication Data

Easum, Bill.
    Leadership on the otherside: no rules, just clues/ Bill Easum.
      p. cm.
    ISBN 0-687-08588-8
    1. Leadership—Religious aspects—Christianity.   I. Title.

BV4597.53.L43 E37 2000
253—dc21

                                  00-044153

Scripture quotations, unless otherwise indicated, are from the *New Revised Standard Version of the Bible,* copyright 1989, Division of Christian Education of the National Council of the Churches of Christ in the United States of America. Used by permission. All rights reserved.

Scripture quotations marked (RSV) are from the *Revised Standard Version of the Bible,* copyright 1946, 1952, 1971 by the Division of Christian Education of the National Council of the Churches of Christ in the United States of America. Used by permission. All rights reserved.

Scripture quotations marked (KJV) are from the King James Version of the Bible.

01 02 03 04 05 06 07 08 09—10 9 8 7 6 5 4 3 2

MANUFACTURED IN THE UNITED STATES OF AMERICA

The OtherSide Website

A special place has been prepared for those of you who purchased this book and want to explore the OtherSide more fully or who wish to discover what we've been learning since publishing this book. That place is **www.easumbandy.com/OtherSide**. You will need to use the OtherSide Password (5364) in order to access the site (Login=OtherSide, Password=5364). The site includes free updates, movies, and opportunities to record your comments. Join me on the OtherSide!

102441

Portals to the OtherSide

Preface

Admission to the Ride

T HE WORLD IS RUNNING OUT OF WORLD-CLASS leaders of the caliber of Nelson Mandela and Billy Graham. Another world-class leader, Mother Teresa, died recently. When Mandela and Graham pass, we may never again experience such people in our lifetime. Why is this the case? Is it because of some character flaw in the generations alive today? Or is it because the nature of our times calls for a different type of leader?

It is my belief that we are entering a world so complicated and so fast paced that it requires something far different from the singular world-class leader. Could it be that the emerging world is geared for a totally new understanding of leadership? I think so. And that is what this book is about—*Leadership on the OtherSide* of the current seismographic shifts under way today. On the way to the OtherSide there are no rules, just clues. Throughout the book I will share some of the clues I've discovered.

This book was written with the help of dozens of fellow travelers on our online forums, including people from the United States, Australia, South Africa, Canada, Great Britain, New Zealand, and Indonesia. As each chapter was written, it was posted online and was reviewed by the following people: David Loar, John Keysell (Wales), Stephen Portner, MaryAnn McConnell, Cathy Townley, Regina Snyder, David Porterfield, Ed Hamshar, Glenn Randall Neubauer, Gary L. Dillensnyder, Darrel Manson, Betty Coffey, Kurt Oheim, Steve Schubart, Susan Buchanan, Karen Clausel, David Harkreader, Ken Haines,

Bob Shank, Eric Bagwell, Lorne Wolfe (Canada), Rob Skirving (Canada), Lee P. Cowherd, Peg Williamson, Jeff Raker, Tom Tumblin, Drew Mountcastle, Mark Tittley (South Africa), Steve Bentley, Andrew Hutchinson, Cy Helm, Katherine E. Brearley, David Miller, Ann Scull (Australia), Thomas Karwaki, Shane Burton, Robin Trebilcock (Australia), Max Palmer (New Zealand), and Elaine P. Storberg.

In addition, a handful of people representing this new understanding of leadership were asked to share their unique perspectives on the emerging new world in which God is calling us to lead. Their responses are shared throughout the book. What you will read represents a world team effort. We hope our work inspires you to become part of what God is bringing about in the world today.

A special section on our website has been set aside just for the readers of this book—**www.easumbandy.com/ OtherSide**. It is a goofy place where one can have fun as well as continue the learning experienced in this book. Bookmark it now.

Before we proceed, I must make a confession. I was born in the midst of Modernity, grew up in the height of Modernity, and pastored during the closing of Modernity. Much of my life has been imprinted by Modernity. So talking about the OtherSide of Modernity is a stretch for me. I am aware that I am trying to make sense out of what is happening today, while carrying a lot of baggage from Modernity. But so are many other church leaders who have spent most of their lives under the influence of Christendom and Modernity but who sense the need to reinterpret their ministry in light of what is happening today (Christendom and Modernity will be explained later). To some, I may appear to be seeing "through a glass darkly" at the moment, but at least I am looking through the glass trying to get a glimpse of the OtherSide.

I do have one experience that connects me with the emerging world—I didn't grow up in the church or under much of its influence. I had not read a Bible before the age of sixteen or been to church except once or twice at Easter.

I don't claim to have any definitive answers about leadership on the OtherSide, but I have discovered some clues. I offer them as possible handles for church leaders to grab hold of as we take one of the wildest rides in the history of humankind.

Bill Easum
Port Aransas, Texas, at the dawn
of the new millennium
www.easumbandy.com
easum@easumbandy.com

Leadership on the OtherSide

We are about to witness an explosion of entities built on relationships and technology that will rival the early days of life on Earth.

—Kevin Kelly

In the beginning God created the heavens and the earth. The earth was without form and void, and darkness was upon the face of the deep; and the Spirit of God was moving over the face of the waters.

—Genesis 1:1-2 RSV

My Story Could Be Your Story
The Importance of Life Metaphors

What does leadership mean when:

- we live in a time when the old rules are disappearing and new ones have not yet emerged?
- leadership means asking people to give up old values that have served them well?
- time, place, and form no longer matter?
- everything is deconstructing and decentralizing?

- the way people receive and process knowledge is changing?
- denominationalism is undergoing a metamorphosis?
- everything about the world into which we were born is giving way to a totally new order?

That is the subject of this book.

I was not born a leader. Quite the opposite. I exhibited nothing through junior high that would suggest any leadership aptitude—no set skills or gifts or desire to do much of anything. Consider the following obstacles I faced: I was dyslexic, an extremely slow reader, a strong introvert, the last person chosen for the sandlot baseball team with grades so poor I almost didn't graduate from high school and a poor self-image as a child and youth. I remember one English teacher telling me that I would never amount to much because I couldn't spell "kat." The first time I tried to preach, I made three attempts and then sat down totally defeated.

Over the next few years, I changed denominations twice, leaving me with no "homeboy" networks. I dropped out of the first seminary I attended while working on a doctorate degree. I entered law school because I had given up on the prospect of following the call, but the call was too great. I applied to another seminary and initially was not allowed to enter. Instead, I was made to audit the courses so I could be observed. I went through the entire postgraduate degree as an auditor, not knowing if I would be accepted. It was not until three days before graduation, after I had passed my orals and been asked if I might want to join the seminary faculty, that I was admitted as a student and allowed to graduate. I was admitted then only because my supervising professor intervened on my behalf.

During my early years of ministry, I followed my supervisor's advice and spent most of my first year as a pastor simply getting to know the people. It did not take me long to realize the stupidity of that advice. If I was going to give spiritual leadership among God's people, much less make disciples, I was going to have to grow new skills and gifts. With God's help and many mistakes, my ability to assert myself and take responsibility for leadership began to blossom. My self-esteem also grew as I felt God working in my life and I began to see others grow in their relationship to God. All the time a still small voice kept saying, "You can do this. You can do this."

During my early years of ministry at the church where I served Christ for twenty-four years, my peers continually told me I was crazy because of the way I did ministry. My supervisors were always "on my case" because I was not following the denomination's way of doing things. Many of my peers referred to me as "the maverick," a term I came to cherish. In time, people began asking me what I was doing that caused the church in which I served Christ to grow. Now I travel a couple of hundred days a year sharing what I've learned.

What grew me into a leader? Two things—my conversion and a burning passion for others to experience Christ as I have.

First, I was transformed from no belief to belief in Jesus Christ, from a poor self-image to a self-image as "made in the image of God." At the age of sixteen, I began to interpret *my* story in light of *the* story, and Jesus Christ began his wonderful work in me. It has been an awesome ride ever since. For someone who did not grow up in the church, this was what could only be interpreted as a turning point for all that would later happen in my life.

This conversion literally rewired the way I felt, thought, and behaved. My view of reality itself changed. Throughout the book, I will refer to this rewiring as a change in our Life Metaphors.[1] *Life Metaphors are the unwritten and mostly unconscious assumptions, rules, and prejudices that form the basis of how we feel, think, and act.* These Life Metaphors are the sum total of all of our experiences—

what we've read, been told, seen, heard, and felt. They define who we are and what we do. They are the "been there, done that" of our lives.

Everyone perceives reality through their Life Metaphors. Based on them, "life is good" or "life is hard" or "it don't matter" or "life stinks." Our Life Metaphors are more important for shaping our existence than the material facts that surround our lives. We are our Life Metaphors. This book is about how our Life Metaphors shape our ministry.

Life Metaphors are different from a worldview. Life Metaphors construct reality for us rather than simply organize it. They create the world we inhabit rather than simply describe it. Much more than just a worldview is at stake. How we construct reality itself is involved in our Life Metaphors. When our Life Metaphors change, we change.

My conversion totally rewired my Life Metaphors. It would take some time before I understood how crucial this experience was in the shaping of my leadership abilities.

Perhaps a conversion is what you need. I am not casting doubt on your faith, but one of the things I am discovering on my own journey is that very often before a person can lead, he or she has to have what is very close to a conversion experience—not redemptive in nature, but just as fundamental and life-altering as salvation itself and so fundamental that it rewires our Life Metaphors.

After my conversion, life itself took on new meaning. People began to notice a difference in my life. "So if anyone is in Christ, there is a new creation: everything old has passed away; see, everything has become new! All this is from God, who reconciled us to himself through Christ, and has given us the ministry of reconciliation" (2 Cor. 5:17-18). Isn't it wonderful to know that God can use people who were chosen last? Perhaps there is still something God is calling you to do with your life. Perhaps you are the next Mandela or Graham.

LEADERSHIP CLUE:

Leaders are obedient to a call greater than their own lives.

This clue is the foundation of all other clues. It is one of only two clues that are present in every spiritual leader I've known. In a sense, one can say that being a leader is about doing what has to be done in order for the mission to be accomplished (more on the mission later).

My greatest living mentor is my friend Dick Wills, pastor of Christ United Methodist Church in Fort Lauderdale. We seldom have a conversation without being reminded of my need to be more obedient. His people tell me that they constantly see obedience in all that he does. I wish I were more like Dick—my ability to fulfill my call would be much easier and my life much better. Like Jacob, most of us limp a good part of our lives because of our lack of obedience. Whenever I stumble, it is always because I am not obeying my call to help others to make disciples. My guess is you find that to be true also.

I'm finding a lot of demoralized leaders in our churches. Many pastors are leaving ministry or retiring earlier. Many laypeople have given up on any hope of having a thriving church. I'm convinced the primary reason is the absence or loss of a personal mission in life from God that is bigger than their own lives. All most people need to do in such a situation is take their Bible and go off until they get a vision. People with a vision from God don't burn out or become demoralized, they just keep on going and going and going. What's the key?

The key is to withdraw and discover or rediscover what God has called you to do and then equip the priesthood to make that vision happen. If the church in which you currently find yourself does not share that vision, move on until your personal mission and the mission of the church match.

My personal mission statement during all of my ministry has been "I will equip every person to be a minister of Jesus Christ." The only time in my ministry I burned out was when I lost sight of that vision.

What is your personal mission in life and how are you achieving it? Perhaps it is time for you to take stock of where you are in your spiritual journey. If you died today, would you feel good about what you have accomplished? Would you hear God say, "Well done, my good and faithful servant"? Could it be that you are just treading water?

Second, I felt called by God to do a mission that required much more of me than had surfaced in my life. If I was to pursue God's call to make disciples, I had no choice but to grow beyond what I was at the moment. I had to make straight A's my last year in high school just to graduate. I had to find a college that would take me with barely passing grades. I had to learn how to read more than seventy-five words a minute in order to keep up with the course load. I had to fight my way out of one denominational system and into another. God had to have something for me to do and it was up to me to find out what it was.

I grew into being a leader when my Life Metaphors changed. These new Life Metaphors changed my images about the basics of life. It was only then that I could hear God calling me to do something with my life. All through the struggle, God supplied whatever I needed to follow the call. I believe that God has a "call" for every Christian.

I was not a visionary leader. I'm still not as visionary as I would like to be. But I evolved into a visionary leader, and so can you.

This book is based on the premise that all people with a call from God can be leaders when they exercise the *spiritual gifts* given to them by God.[2] If you're not a leader, there's hope for you. Your hope will b e found in the rewiring of your Life Metaphors.

Three observations can be drawn from my story.
1. God can use those whom others choose last.
2. No one knows who will or won't be a leader.
3. Almost anyone who wants it badly enough can be a leader!

Before reading on, think back to the time when you first began your Christian journey. Form an image of that time in your life. Remember how you felt?—the naive passion, the dreams, the unlimited way you threw yourself into the journey? Has your passion waned over the years? Perhaps it has been beaten out of you by a cold sterile system of church government. Layperson, perhaps you've bought into the myth that you're "just a layperson." Clergyperson, perhaps seminary took the mystery out of most things that caused your spine to tingle in those first years of your Christian journey. Perhaps all you need is to rediscover those feelings that have been smothered and buried in the past few years.

Leaders surrender to something bigger than their own lives. They know their destiny is to create God's new future, to continually change the status quo, to create environments in which people spiritually mature. They intuitively know that God will provide whatever they need to fulfill their destiny. So their primary purpose is to place themselves at the center of what God is doing in history. Their prayer is, "Lord, put me in the center of your will. Let me bless what you are doing." Spiritual giants do not feel the need to invoke God's presence, so they don't ask God to be present. They know God is always "with them." Like the Latin phrase says, "Invoked or not invoked, God is present."

The leaders I have observed have a sense of destiny that continually draws out of them more than even they see in themselves. They sense that they are participating in an awesome adventure alongside of God, helping to alter the course of human history. It never enters their minds that something is impossible. They base their lives on the premise that with God all things can be accomplished. Therefore, they are always stretching themselves to deeper levels of faith. In a sense, they have a holy discontent with the status quo.

Image and Story

Each of us has a story that shapes our image of life. This image goes a long way toward determining our behavior. Until recently, the story that has shaped most church leaders has gone something like this:

The universe is like a giant clock created by a master clock builder and left to wind down. Matter is the basic building block of life. Everything else is not real. People are little more than extremely complicated machines whose purpose is to produce goods for others to consume. Expanding consumption is the goal of enterprise. We should not worry about running out of resources because the universe, along with all of our institutions, is dying anyway. That is the natural order according to Sir Issac Newton.

As a result of this story, church leaders often: revere institutions as much as if not more than the God they profess to love; work to preserve those institutions often at the expense of humanity; design those institutions around policies, money, bureaucracies, and hierarchies; and above all, seek to keep the precious institutions under tight control. Even when those institutions no longer achieve what they were created to do, because of the story, church leaders live and breathe to keep them open.

However, a new story is being written today that a handful of church leaders are beginning to sing. Because of the discovery of quantum mechanics,[3] we know that Sir Issac didn't know all of the story. The rules of mechanical causality don't apply to everything. The universe is not necessarily winding down. Chaos is always creating something new. Life is more organic than Newton thought. The new song goes something like this:

The universe is a self-organizing system much like a giant garden. It flourishes best when cared for by lov-

ing gardeners who break up the clods, till the soil, and plant the seeds of the future. Spirit is the basic building block of life. Energy and change are the primary ingredients of this universe. Since everything is connected in this universe, creating a nurturing environment is crucial to the well-being of life. Because the universe is always recreating itself, we have just begun to explore our relationship to the creator and to our potential, and we have yet to imagine our destiny. That is the natural order according to quantum mechanics.

As a result of this story, a new breed of leader is emerging today. Their image of reality is shaped by this new story and they seem driven by a sense of spiritual destiny. When I talk with them, I realize I am talking with a different kind of church leader than I have seen before. This book is about them.

Clues Instead of Laws or Principles

I suppose a time may have existed in which one could speak about the laws or principles of leadership. But not now. Not in times like these. There is no one model for leadership—no list of laws or principles. Everything is too tenuous at this stage of the ride for us to talk in terms of absolutes (except for one thing that we will learn later).

So throughout the book, I will share *clues* about leadership instead of *laws* or *principles.* When clues are shared, ask yourself, "How does this apply to my life?" Try to experience the metaphor in the clue. Think of leadership as an art rather than a science.

By concentrating on the following clues, it is my hope that the reader will be able to see between the lines and beneath the words. The clues will help you connect the dots, see the trends, and anticipate what might be coming your way. These clues are in no way predictions, just a Wizard to help you construct a template for your own style of leadership.[4]

An Important Question for Our Time

In every major organization around the world, one question dominates the boardroom: "How do we develop the leaders we need for these uncertain times?" When everyone is asking the same question at the same time, you know something of great importance is taking shape. Every area of life is in desperate need of leaders who can lead in a world of uncertainty.

The church is no exception. The greatest challenge of our times is to develop leaders who can function effectively when all of the rules are changing. How these leaders feel and think and act in uncertain times is the subject of this book.

One of the primary questions of our time is, *If leadership is the greatest challenge of the twenty-first century, and if this new century is going to be radically different, what kind of leaders do we need to begin growing today so the church can thrive in the twenty-first century?* This book is an attempt to address that question.

Who This Book Is Really For

This book is for Christians who love their Christ, their church, and their community so much that they yearn for every individual to experience the transforming power of Christ and to grow into the full stature of Christ. It is not for church leaders who merely want to take care of people or who only care for those they can personally bring to Christ or help grow in their faith or who are busy checking the membership statistics.

What is the difference between the above two types of leaders? Leaders of the first type allow a church to grow beyond their ability to love and nurture it; leaders of the second type keep the church small and dependent on them. The first depicts secure, whole individuals who love to see others outgrow their need of them; the second depicts persons who can't or won't allow people to out-grow their need of them. The first depicts the average pastor of many growing churches in the world; the second depicts the pastor in the average declining church in the world. The first is a picture of how Jesus trained his disciples; the second is a picture of how too many pastors function. The first grows healthy, independent, and inter-connected people who live out their own spiritual gifts; the second grows unhealthy, dependent people who rely on their leader to do ministry for them. A universe of difference exists between these two types of leaders.

In the thriving church of the future the primary role of every leader will be to provide an environment in which people can grow to be disciples who grow other disciples. They will live and breathe helping others grow in their faith, rather than merely taking care of them. True, some people need to be taken care of. However, most people have within them so much to share with others. Many are just waiting for the opportunity to stretch their spiritual wings and birth their gifts. Church leaders who truly care about them give them that opportunity instead of keeping them dependent.

What to Expect

This is not a book about the future. It is about what is happening right now and the implications for leadership at the turn of the century. What is happening, you ask? We are entering a period of deconstruction in which

Christendom and Modernity are coming to an end (more on these later). At the moment, nothing has replaced either and probably nothing will for several decades. We are truly in a crack in history. Most writers refer to this crack as "postmodern." I will avoid the use of the term.[5] I prefer the term "pre-Christian," which I will explain later.

Like the emerging world, not everyone will read this book in the same media. Some will curl up with it in the familiar bound book form. Others will download it from our website and view it on screen. Some will choose to view the animated graphics on the website prepared just for this book at **www.easumbandy. com/OtherSide**. Others will be content simply viewing the static graphics provided in the bound book. Still others will invest in online conversations with me. The more adventurous will surf the many websites scattered throughout the book and endnotes. Such is the unfolding richness of our world.

I invite you to join in the dialogue and not just read the book. Explore the many ramifications of the thoughts and feelings evoked in you while reading. Push the author through the e-mail opportunity provided on the OtherSide website and do the exercises at the end of each section.

Perhaps some budding web afficionado will create an interactive experience and add it to the site. Someone else may decide to improve the graphics and exchange them for the ones we've designed. So be it. Go for it. Expand it. Improve it. To do so may be your step to the OtherSide.

Getting Ready for the OtherSide

Leaders on the OtherSide of the current cultural revolution grow leaders who grow leaders. The emerging world needs leaders of leaders, not leaders and followers.

Let me drive home this point. **Everyone has the potential to be a leader. We must dispel the belief in the heroic leader who single-handedly saves the day.** If I can be a leader, so can you.

Join me on a journey of experiencing how this new breed of leader feels, thinks, and acts—and how you can be a leader on the OtherSide.

Journal Entries and Other Painfully Wonderful Experiences to Help You Feel and Think

1. You'll find it helpful to begin a personal journal to record your feelings and thoughts as you read. Toward the end of the book you'll be asked to refer back to your original entries to see if you sense any change in how you perceive ministry.

2. How do you feel about my personal story? Did you find anything in it that speaks to you personally? Did if offer any hints about what you might do to become a better leader?

3. Describe the first time you felt God's presence in your life.

4. Reread the first Leadership Clue on page 17. Do you have such a call? If so, how would you describe it? If not, how would you describe the reason you are reading this book? What does your discovery suggest might be helpful to you?

5. Develop your own personal mission statement. What is it that you are willing to spend your life accomplishing? *The Path* by Laurie Beth Jones is a good book that can help in this process.[6]

6. How would you describe your role in your church— one who takes care of people or one who goes to meetings or one who equips others to be disciples of Jesus Christ? Is this the role you prefer?

7. Do you agree with the statement "Everyone has the potential to be a leader"? Can you see how this

would change the way church leaders relate to everyone in the church if church leaders believed it?

8. Now is a good time to go to **www.easumbandy.com/ OtherSide** and see what it can offer you.

Leadership Clues to the Wormhole

The Leader's Cheat Sheet

Leadership on the OtherSide

1. Leaders are obedient to a call greater than their own lives.

The Challenge of Our Times

2. Leaders on the OtherSide feel passionately about a few core issues and think paradoxically about most other things.

Into the Wormhole

3. Leaders are keenly aware of their need to be led intuitively by the Holy Spirit.
4. Leaders are constantly innovating "on the fly."

The Death of Two Kissing Cousins

5. Leaders know how to share Jesus with pagans.

The Mother Life Metaphor

6. Leaders sense that the basic genetic code of the church is to make disciples of Jesus Christ.

Spiritual Guides: Explorers of the OtherSide

7. Leaders function as spiritual directors or guides.
8. Leaders feel and think like cross-cultural witnesses.

The Lone Ranger Was a Team Player

9. Leaders are permission-giving.
10. Leaders are team-based.

Whose Church Is It, Anyway?

11. Leaders serve Jesus Christ in the midst of a congregation instead of serving a congregation.

Almost to the OtherSide

12. It's not what leaders know that is important; it's what leaders know is not important.
13. Leaders need a clear sense of what it means to be human.
14. Leaders need to be able to help others distinguish reality from fiction.

Remain Seated with Your Seat
Belt Buckled: The Ride's Not Over

15. Leaders are willing to change their Life Metaphors.

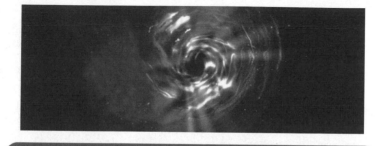

Portal 1

The Challenge of Our Times

We are all born to manifest the glory of God in all of us.
—Nelson Mandela

The significant problems we face cannot be solved at the same level of thinking we were at when we created them.
—Albert Einstein

The salvation of the soul lies in the human heart.
—Vaclav Havel

Every transformation of [humans]. . . has rested on a new metaphysical and ideological base; or rather, upon deeper stirrings and intuitions whose rationalized expressions take the form of a new picture of the cosmos and of [humanity].
—Lewis Mumford

MY HOPE IS TO PASS ON ONE OF THE GREATEST lessons I've observed in life: leaders who are growing disciples today *feel, think,* and *act* differently than leaders of the past. They're gripped by a different view of reality. They see what most people cannot or will not see. Curiosity oozes from them. They have deep passion about what they do. They think off the wall and outside of the box. They seem able to paint into being what most people cannot even imagine. They exist in a different dimension. Their comments and actions often scare people who have not assumed the mantle of leadership or who lead by control or rules. In every respect, today's leaders are very different from most leaders throughout the history of Christendom.[1]

Many of these leaders are under the age of thirty and you have never heard of them. They are the quiet new breed of everyday leaders who do not always stand out from the crowd. They simply go about their mission doing what they are called to do.

These leaders are wired differently than in the past. They have an altered genetic code. Change the genetic code and you change what a person is capable of seeing, hearing, feeling, and doing. In radically shifting times, changing the way a person feels and thinks is the key to a nonleader becoming a leader. "As he [she] thinketh in his [her] heart, so is he [she]" (Proverbs 23:7 KJV).

LEADERSHIP CLUE:

Leaders feel passionately about a few core issues and think paradoxically about most other things.

To feel deeply about a few core issues (referred to later as DNA) and to be able to accept and use the yin and the yang[2] of most everything else is the key to leadership in the twenty-first century. The ability to focus as well as to embrace two sides of the same coin is basic to the leader's intersection with reality. Leaders have to have an intense passion about the core issues and an amazing flexibility with everything else.

Leaders see beyond either/or solutions and embrace the mystery of metaphor, the paradox of both/and, the mysticism of symbol, and the open-ended nature of visuals. They go beyond the rational and analytical to the heart and song of their own life's ritual. More than tell the story, they become the story. More than explain the message, they experience with the fellow traveler the story, the vibration, and the song of the metanarrative. Rather than explain, they enact the story.

To leaders, meaning is conveyed through experience. They seldom see their role as mediator between God and humanity. Their role is to bring the two together. The leadership challenge facing most pastors and church officials at the dawn of a new millennium is learning how to shake loose, innovate, and merge the depths of our mental and emotional sensibilities. In a word, to tap the primitive and primal.

The King James version of Proverbs 23:7 shares with us the heart of the leader on the OtherSide, "For as he [she] thinketh in his [her] heart, so is he [she]." I love the image of "thinking in the heart." What a metaphor! But this is exactly how these leaders respond to the world around them. They equally feel and think, but they lead with their heart. Their emotions are allowed to run wild and mix with their thinking until it is impossible to tell where one ends and the other begins—a difficult task for most Western/European-oriented people born prior to 1965.

I have a stock answer to many questions: "If you want it badly enough, you can do it." Of all the human characteristics that go into the making of a leader, none is as important as one's *passion* for the mission. Every authentic leader I have known has a deep, burning passion to change the way things are instead of just taking care of people. These folks live to change lives. It pervades everything they do and say. One pastor told me, "There's nothing more fulfilling in life than to see a person come to faith and begin to grow as a Christian, and then see that person help someone else have the same experience." This passion is so strong that it can overcome a host of inadequate skills. I know a pastor who didn't graduate from high school, who butchers the King's English, and still leads one of the largest churches in America.

The key to developing this passion is in seeing the difference between changing lives and taking care of people. Most leaders I've met would rather change lives than care for lives. Such an attitude does not mean that they don't care about people. They care so much about people that the last thing they want to do is to make anyone dependent on them for care. They want to grow people, and the first step in spiritual growth is change.

Because of this burning passion to change lives, leaders are able to remain focused on the core issues regardless of the distractions. It is also passion that allows them to be flexible in noncrucial matters. The tragedy is that too many would-be leaders lack passion for the mission and they lose their focus and/or concentrate on minor issues. The best way I know to describe this combination of passion, focus, and perseverence is to share a personal story.

A few years back, I felt a call to enter the world of consulting. Over a four-year period I received several nudges from congregations to come and share what we were learning in the church where I had pastored for two decades. I discussed these nudges with some trusted leaders of the church and they suggested I pursue them while remaining their pastor. There was just one catch to this plan. The time came when the places I had to go to were too far to drive and I had to take a plane. At this point in my life I had been on a plane only once, at the age of four, when I took a trip with my mother. The wings froze and the plane broke up upon landing, leaving me with a deep-seated fear of flying.

For the next two years of consulting I had to take tranquilizers just to get on a plane. I went through several bottles of tranquilizers in order to get to my consultations. Finally I said, "Enough. I have no choice. I have to fly. The mission demands it. But I can't continue this way. What am I to do?"

The answer to my dilemma was simple—I had to learn to fly. So I took flying lessons and a year later earned my pilot's license. I still remember my first solo flight. On final approach, I said to myself, "This one's for the mission." It took a year more before I could say, "This one's for me." To this day I still can't sleep on a plane, but I've thrown away the tranquilizers, and the mission continues. Why? Because my passion for the mission was stronger than my fear of flying. I felt as if I didn't have a choice. How deep is your passion for changing individual lives and society?

The Problem at the End of the Millennium

Today leaders are called upon to feel deeply. And here is the kicker—they will think through their feelings.

Most of today's laity function as care takers and givers rather than spiritual leaders—going to endless rounds of meaningless meetings, trying to manage and protect decaying institutions from extinction. Most of today's pastors function as chaplains—going about taking care of people, visiting shut-ins and hospitals, serving communion, and mouthing archaic rituals understood by a decreasing number of people. This shouldn't be. These ministries are important, but they are not the responsibility of the pastor. That's not biblical.[3] These ministries are the responsibility of all the people of God.

God calls everyone to some form of gifted leadership that builds up the Body of Christ.[4] However, our systems, rules, and policies keep us from discovering our leadership gifts. Most of our seminaries teach us to be theologians, chaplains, and managers instead of spiritual leaders. Pastors right out of seminary often become associate pastors and are taught how to manage or chaplain by the senior pastor. Many leaders of today have been shut down or turned off by the present way of "doing" church. This shouldn't be. God is calling every Christian to birth the God-given gifts within them, but the response of the institutional church is restricting and squelching our response.

The Essence of Postmodern Leadership
Brad Sargent

Who—We postmoderns think in webs of relationships and multiple layers of meaning. We offer the Church a gift of rejuvenation in a confusing culture that has more in common with the pagan first century than with all the Enlightenment era. We can stand on the verge of chaos and complexity and find it energizing instead of frightening. We can sit with people in all their emotional pain and not be in a rush to get them into a self-help healing program; the wounds were relational, and informational solutions alone will never be enough to remove the brokenness. We can live within the paradoxical tension of wanting to influence the world yet often seeing that our lives are lived in small arenas. But we persevere because God has called us to be God's faithful servants, not successful servants.

Situation—We are so very different from moderns in the way we process information and in many of the things we value. There are so many bases from which we could derive conflict! And we have done our share of blaming and shaming. We long for unity, as moderns do, but we also believe we must act with authenticity and integrity to be who God has created us to be for just such a time as this. Please persevere with us if we conclude we have to do something new in order to obey God, even if it is without your understanding or blessing. Please share your fellowship and wisdom with us as we engage in new endeavors for God's kingdom. Please pray for us as the Spirit of Christ launches us out from and into a multicultural world, much like he did from ancient Antioch in the book of Acts.

Biggest Challenges--judgmentalism, self-pity, intolerance. As postmoderns called by God into leadership, we must distinguish between valid critique and judgmentalism. Jesus came to us full of grace and truth—both/and, not either/or--so we must make every effort to maintain the bond of unity in peace with members of the Body of Christ from all generations and from all mind-sets. We can never excuse any disobedience on our part by attributing it to our being held back by moderns. And we must also realize that we are no more monolithic in our culture than are moderns. We postmoderns range from mild to wild, and church will not look the same for all of us simply because we hold to some degree of postmodern stuff! So we must overcome our own ironic intolerance, and give one another the freedom to follow biblical principles within our varying degrees of postmodern values and perspectives, always encouraging one another to be Bereans (Acts 17:11) and check it out for ourselves in scripture.

Best Opportunities--three strategic roles; a real, relational, and realistic incarnational ministry approach. There are at least three strategic ministry roles that postmoderns can do best: mission strategy coordinators for unreached people and groups; hard-core urban ministers; and pioneers of indigenous, reproducible church-planting movements. All three rely on such abilities as toleration for high degrees of ambiguity and creation of layered, holistic ministry responses to exceptionally complex personal, social, and cultural problems. Our organic, systemic ways of thinking (not just the analytic, systematic ways of moderns) will help us contextualize the truth into breathtaking new paradigms that meet other postmoderns where they are in their spiritual journeys.

Also, we know that "our tribes" in this postmodern world like a good story. We seek to give them more than a snatch of Christ's story embodied again in our personage as the ultimate apologetic. And we have the best metanarrative in the universe to offer those who do not yet realize that this is what (actually

Whom) they are really searching for in all their spiritual quests. With God's leading and the blessings of our community of faith, we are ready to rock the world--even if we pray globally and act locally!

Brad Sargent works at Golden Gate Baptist Theological Seminary as a project developer and writer/editor and serves at Bay Marin Community Church in San Rafael, California. Brad is a postmodern trapped in a boomer body.[5]

Why do our systems create and perpetuate the conditions that are causing their own downfall? Why do so many of our leaders continue to do and say the same old things expecting that, by some miracle, the same old efforts or thoughts will result in something different happening than has happened in the past?

Although there are numerous theories as to why systems continue to perpetuate the status quo,[6] for our purposes it boils down to how Western/Europeans view reality. Our Life Metaphors are getting in the way. We break reality into bits and pieces and focus on isolated individuals and linear cause and effect. As a result, we neither see the big picture nor the interrelated loopiness of the whole system.[7]

In the last ten years, I have observed eight Life Metaphors that dominate the leadership of our time. These Life Metaphors either inspire or deter us from being leaders. I'll list them now and discuss each one in depth later. For now, view the following Life Metaphors as if they were traveling through a portal from the world in which you were born to the new world that is emerging all around us. In the next chapter, I will describe this portal as a wormhole through which all of us are passing.

As we travel into this new world, the items below represent blurred fragments of a paradoxical environment spiraling toward the future. **Do not view them as opposites or contrasts, or as good and bad.**

"What Was" Life Metaphors	"What is Emerging" Life Metaphors
Matter	Spirit
Mechanical	Organic
Institutional	Spiritual
Church	Kin-dom
Committees	Teams
Entitled and Elected	Called Servants
European Command and Control	Indigenous Permission Giving
Command and Control	Permission Giving

Churches need a 12-step group for those addicted to old forms. "Hi, my name is Bill. I attend this church because I know it is the one place in my life where nothing is ever going to change."

One Possible Solution

Churches wanting to break free from the quagmire of their dysfunctional systems and climb out of their downward death spiral must learn to feel, think, and act differently than they do now. The times in which we live require us to change our Life Metaphors, something akin to rewiring the human brain.[8]

For half a century, researchers have been studying the way the mind works. It seems our minds make decisions based on unconscious routines (that is, Life Metaphors). These Life Metaphors determine how we shift through the bites and pieces of reality that flood through our senses every day. When confronted with a decision, we draw on these Life Metaphors to help us solve the problem. The more complex the problem, the more helpful or harmful these Life Metaphors can be.

Over a long period of cultural stability, our Life Metaphors become anchors that firmly ground our decision-making processes. Given this situation, we intuitively know what our response should be until we encounter cultural instability like we are experiencing today (the subject of the next chapter). In times of great instability our Life Metaphors often become liabilities. When what worked yesterday backfires today, we short-circuit and become paralyzed. The longer this action continues, the less likely we are to make even the most simple decisions. In time, the organization becomes leaderless. That's where we are today.

Most churches resemble a person who has just received a life-threatening blow to the head. Because of the trauma, the body systems begin to shut down one after the other until finally all that remains is a shell of what used to be.

Are your Life Metaphors anchors that hold you in place or portals to a new way of perceiving reality?

In his groundbreaking book *Emotional Intelligence,* Daniel Goleman performs a great service to the field of leadership.[9] I have always believed that passion is the most important trait of any effective leader, but I didn't know why until I read this book. Goleman's conclusion is that emotional intelligence matters more in leadership than IQ.

Goleman bases his conclusion on the architecture of the human brain. It seems as if the human brain develops in three separate stages. The brain stem, which controls our involuntary actions like heartbeat and reflexes, develops first. The limbic system, which controls our emotions, develops around the brain stem much later. The cortex and neocortex, which are the center for complex thinking, develop last, long after the limbic system.

Research shows that we respond to stimuli in the same stages that our brain develops. The limbic system, which stores all of our emotional memory, seems to occupy a privileged position in the brain. It has a direct connection to our thalamus, which processes all incoming sensory information. We *feel* about all stimuli before we *think* about them. I hope you are seeing all kinds of implications for leadership.

We scan everything that happens to us through our emotions. *We feel before we think.* We want to see if what we are experiencing correlates to any good or bad feelings in our past experiences. Have you ever said, "I wish I hadn't said that"? You acted on your feelings, then your intellect kicked in and you felt awful. Leaders on the Otherside won't do this.

Here's the problem. Over the last five or six decades, many church leaders have been brainwashed into believing that how one *thinks* about one's faith is more important than how one *feels* about one's faith. In today's world that is suicide!

The challenge for leadership is to change the way we feel and think about all the stimuli that bombard us every day, not to try harder or to spend more money on things that no longer work. For some of us, this means giving more credence to the feeling side of our faith, to appeal to the heart as well as the head, to not be afraid to share our emotions as well as our thoughts, to be as comfortable with the dramatic Damascus Road conversions as with the Emmaus Road conversions that evolve over longer periods of time, to place as much and even more emphasis on experience as on information.

Leadership has more to do with helping people feel again about their faith than with solving problems. We don't need to work harder; we need to have a different view of work. We don't need a better structure; we need to change the architecture of our brain. We don't need to worry about our problems; we need to get a new pair of glasses so we can see things from a different perspective.

Before we can change the way we act, we have to change the way we feel and think. We have to change our image of reality. We have to change the way we perceive the church. That is the purpose of this book—to help church leaders change the way they feel and think and therefore act.

I want to mess with your mind! I want to help you change the way you feel and think about the word "church." So form an image of what comes to mind when you feel and think about the word "church." Before reading on, record your feelings. If possible, draw a picture of that image. Write down a set of metaphors that help you express this image.

As we progress through the book and explore the eight basic Life Metaphors of church, it will become clear how they determine most of the way we give or withhold leadership. But above all, enjoy the ride to the OtherSide.

Journal Entries and Other Painfully Wonderful Experiences to Help You Feel and Think

1. Close your eyes and form an image of the word "church." What do you see? Write it down. Use an animal, vegetable, or mineral to describe it. Why not send me the results at **easum@easumbandy.com**?

2. In one sitting, read the Acts of the Apostles to get a feel for the churches in the first century. While doing so, what images of "church" do you get? Write them down. How do these images compare to the church in which you find yourself? Do you like or dislike the comparisons? What feelings does it evoke? What do you see? Can you draw a picture of what you saw? What do your images say to you about how you think and feel about your church?

3. Which of the following images of the church do you resonate with the best?

   "The church is like a home with every style of architecture imaginable."

   "The church is like an art gallery in which there are pictures from every era possible."

   This first image describes how many ineffective leaders feel about the postmodern world. The second describes how postmoderns feel about their world.

4. Tell the story of your life in the church and its importance or unimportance to you. Discuss it with a friend.

5. What is your dream for your church?

6. Look at the words describing the world that was and the world that is emerging. Form an image of both sides. Which side best describes your church? Which do you think is most biblical? What scriptures can you think of that support your claim?

7. In this chapter, I talked about my call to consulting. Have you ever had the feeling that God is calling you to do something very different with your life than anything you have done so far? What has kept you from responding? What needs to happen before you can respond positively?

8. Watch an episode of *The Brady Bunch* and then an episode of *Seinfeld.* What differences do you see and what does it tell you about where we are headed?

9. How do you feel about the way leadership is described in this chapter? Does it make you feel good or bad? Happy or depressed?

10. What do you think your church needs to do to provide such leadership?

11. In this chapter, I said that one of the greatest needs of our time is for leaders who can grow other leaders. If that is so, how much money and time does your church spend developing leaders? Do you need to change your focus? Do you need to put more money into continuing education?

12. Which part of the brain do you use the most—feeling or thinking? Which would you prefer to use more? What is stopping you from doing so?

Portal 2

Into the Wormhole

Matter . . . . Spirit

Every few hundred years in Western history, there occurs a sharp transition. Within a few short decades, society rearranges itself—its worldview; its basic values; its social and political structure; its arts; its key institutions. Fifty years later, there is a new world. And the people born then cannot imagine the world in which their grandparents lived and into which their own parents were born. We are currently living through just such a transformation.

—Peter Drucker

IMAGINE YOU'RE SPIRALING INWARD, AROUND AND around, twisting and turning, pitchpoling head over heels, through a chaotic and soundless maze of lights and swirls toward an unknown destination. Your heart feels as if it's about to leap out of your body. Your head feels the size of a watermelon. You're not sure you can survive much more and you're tempted to abort the ride. Miraculously, you emerge from the chaos, still alive and in one piece. You're on the OtherSide.

Life Today Is Like a Wild Ride

You and I are a part of something *big.* Our world is plunging head over heels through a remarkable period of history. The epistemological, philosophical, ontological, and metaphysical structures underlying all of our belief and values systems are coming apart and being reassembled. As a result, the way people process knowledge is undergoing a profound metamorphosis of mind and heart.[1] Something of this magnitude happens only once or twice a millennium.

This change of mind and heart is occurring so rapidly and relentlessly that many of today's leaders are paralyzed with fright. Their hearts can't take the ride, so they're resigned to a slow, agonizing death of spirit. Such fear among church leaders has never been experienced before, not even while some of our predecessors burned at the stake. It's life-threatening if you are a person who tends to think more than you feel.

Life Today Is Like a Wormhole

Scientists have a word for this kind of ride. They call it a "wormhole." A wormhole is thought to be a portal in space that offers rapid travel from one universe to another.

Wormhole is my metaphor for the present transition to a new epoch of history.[2] We are going through a fundamental change in the rules of the game of life—a time of radical discontinuity—passing through a wormhole to the OtherSide of somewhere. Like East Berliners the day after the wall came down, nothing has prepared most of us for life on the OtherSide. All of the established rules are disappearing and the new rules are still a blur. The discontinuity is so rapid and so all-encompassing that many are beginning to concede that it will be impossible to preserve many of our existing institutions.

To understand this metaphor, take a yardstick and a tape measure three feet long. Look at the yardstick. It is clear that the shortest distance from zero inches to the three-foot point is exactly three feet. Now spread the tape measure out on the floor. Again, the shortest distance between these two points is clearly three feet. But now pick up the tape measure and roll it up by looping it back and forth every five inches or so. Now how far is it from the zero inch mark to the end? It isn't three feet, is it? It is about four or five times the width of the tape measure, really quite small. Such is a wormhole in theory.

Speed is a key word in the wormhole. Scientists believe that possibly our universe is constructed more like a tape measure than like a yardstick. If they are correct, then it may well be possible to travel through vast distances in space by traveling through a "wormhole" where points are "looped" together. The distances involved are so vast that a space traveler would emerge in a part of space that we cannot even see from earth with our most sophisticated instruments.[3]

The rate of change is always greater in between epochs. As a new epoch becomes established, the change slows and becomes evolutionary instead of revolutionary. It has always been that way in history and nothing suggests that it will change. The only difference today is that the pattern of behavior in the wormhole is so rapid and continuously in flux that we are experiencing revolutionary discontinuity. We are not slowly evolving into a new world, we are experiencing what can be compared to a rift in the cosmos—a wormhole.

The making of great epochs of history has taken centuries in the past. However, because of the rapid rate of change today, the making of this new age will take much less time. Like computers progressing at lightning speed compared to the advance of the automobile, so the wormhole will close and the new rules will be written much more quickly than the making of any other period of history.

"Blur" is also a key word in the wormhole. The blurring of boundaries is at the heart of this wild ride.[4] The speed at which we are moving causes everything to appear as one big blur. Things that were once clear are now up for grabs.

Life in the wormhole is like the Exile. We are strangers in a new world where all of the reliable rules and structures are missing and we are no longer in control. Like the Hebrews, we'll learn that God is present even in the wormhole. Like the Hebrews, to survive we'll develop a counterstance to the new culture and not bow to the gods of the empire. If the wormhole is like the Exile, we can expect some of our most creative literature and theological conversations to emerge over the next few years.

In a world ruled by speed, the longer it takes a church to make a decision the less accurate and effective the decision is. The time spent deliberating on the decision allows the world to pass your church by. So why annual budgets, annual meetings, quadrennial emphasis, or two-hour staff meetings? Are they all a waste of time moving through the wormhole?

However, the wormhole is about much more than speed and blur. It is also about flux—constant, discontinuous flux. It is the making of a new epoch such as when the Modern Age or the Bronze Age began. By 2015 we will be a bit more clear about the rules of the game.[5] By the midpoint of the next century, people will be looking back and describing the rules. Right now all we can do in a time between rules is look for the clues to the future.

I'll use the image of the wormhole throughout this book. Traveling through the wormhole demands that we leave behind our arrogant assumptions that the church as we know it is the "normal" way for a church to be. God is taking us to a place where "being the church" is quite another thing.

If wormholes do exist, they won't be linear or play by the same rules that we understand on this side. They will spiral in a loopy fashion, much like a double helix. Cause and effect may not exist, at least not as we know them. Greek syllogistic thought will not work in the wormhole. Feeling and thinking are hyperlinked to each other.

Scientists think that whatever passes through the wormhole comes out the OtherSide much different. Some even think that the discontinuity is so pervasive it may be impossible to survive a trip through a wormhole.

But like all metaphors, the wormhole metaphor goes only so far. Whereas wormholes are thought to provide two-way travel, what we're going through today is a one-way ride to a new world. There's no turning back. We can't re-create the 1950s. Denominational attempts at restructuring without changing Life Metaphors are fruitless wastes of time. Trying to revitalize a church without changing the leadership style is useless.

> If the basic assumptions underlying modern society are indeed shifting in the way we have suggested, it follows that society will, only a few generations from now, be as different from modern industrial society as that is from the society of the Middle Ages.[6]

We don't have a choice about whether or not to enter the wormhole. Everything and everyone is being pulled into it. To resist is futile. By resisting we waste precious time and energy. Pretending that nothing is happening leaves us further behind. By holding on to our old cultural assumptions we jeopardize our future. The world does not care what we do. Nor will it wait for us to decide. If you're resisting, pretending, or clinging to old cultural assumptions, the best advice I have for you is, GET OVER IT! For the sake of the gospel, get over it.

Besides, you're in good company in the wormhole—Abraham, Joseph, Moses, Ruth, Jesus, Paul—all had to leave their familiar surroundings to fulfill their God-given call. As always, the scripture has the best advice.

> Do not remember the former things, or consider the things of old. I am about to do a new thing; now it springs forth, do you not perceive it? I will make a way in the wilderness and rivers in the desert. (Isaiah 43:18-19)

Those who successfully make their way through the wormhole will guide us to a very different world, with different rules and worldview. What they build on the way to the OtherSide is the destination. The destination is not something awaiting us, it is what leaders will create as they go.

A New Type of Leader

We can expect two things to occur in our churches over the next two decades. (1) The anger level among church officials will increase, causing more conflict and dysfunctional characteristics. New forms of leadership and worship will be the lightning rods for this anger. (2) We can expect further moral decline and inefficiency to increase among the older clergy. Already, many denominations are beginning to worry more about the legalities of lawsuits than the merits of the Great Commission.

Therefore, a new type of leader is required as we pass through the wormhole. Such leadership has not been seen before in Protestantism. To comprehend the nature of this leadership we must get the prevailing understanding of leadership out of our heads. When I use the word "leader" I do not envision followers who must be convinced to accomplish the leader's vision. Instead, by "leader" I mean someone who encourages and inspires others to reach their own potential as a leader. Leadership is helping people become their best, solve their problems, and make a better world. Leadership is about developing a healthy, vital community of faith. *This book is about leaders of leaders—not followers—because everyone has the potential to lead with his or her God-given gifts.*

No one dominant form of leadership has yet emerged and one probably will not emerge for another decade. We are not far enough into the wormhole to know what kind of leadership will be effective throughout the ride. It would be wise to be leery of those who refer to the laws or rules of leadership. Even Kevin Kelly's book *New Rules for the New Economy* is really not about the rules of leadership as much as it is a powerful list of metaphors about what leadership might be in the future.[7] However, some clues are already emerging.

What Leaders Need to Know Entering The Wormhole

Since this ride is not going to be easy and for some will be unpleasant, a few essentials are helpful to know before being thrust into the wormhole.

The OtherSide Manifesto

1. **Jesus is the only truth we can be sure that we can take into and out of the wormhole.** Jesus is the North Star in the wormhole.

2. **Chaos is the beginning of all new creation.** That is why Jesus said, "And I will ask the Father, and he will give you another Advocate, to be with you forever. This is the Spirit of truth, whom the world cannot receive, because it neither sees him nor knows him. You know him, because he abides with you, and he will be in you. I will not leave you orphaned; I am coming to you" (John 14:16-18).

3. **To be out of control is normal because the wormhole is always under deconstruction.** If you like things nice and neat, you're in for a night of fright or a whale of a migraine.

4. **Our experiences are as important as our thoughts.** Armchair theologians take notice; you're not needed anymore.

5. **Imagination is as important as logical thought.** If you can't help others see it, you won't be able to achieve it.

6. **Questions outnumber answers.** People are looking for guides who will travel with them, not experts.

7. **Constant flux is normal.** Flexibility is a crucial trait.

8. **Because speed is a basic in the wormhole, constant innovation provides equilibrium.** "We've never done it this way before" folk are in for the time of their life.

9. **Most things are upside down and backward.** Dyslexia might help in the wormhole.

10. **The wormhole is not linear.** Those who go around in circles are the leaders of tomorrow.

LEADERSHIP CLUE:

Leaders are keenly aware of their need to be led intuitively by the Holy Spirit.

The wormhole is a chaotic time. That's bad news for church leaders who see chaos as the opposite of order. However, leaders are learning that just the opposite is true. Chaos theory[8] says that instead of the enemy of order and beauty, chaos is an essential early element in the birthing of everything new. Remember that the meeting, not conflict, between chaos and God's Spirit is how God's vision of creation began in the first place (Genesis 1:1).

In the wormhole, leaders sense that the chaotic, unpredictable, and sometimes destructive dynamics of flow are not "tamed" or "controlled" by rules, resolutions, or policies. This is truly counterintuitive. Instead, they are shaped into God's vision by a stronger flow yet. Only one force is stronger than chaos. Only the flow of the Spirit is adequate to meet the chaotic conditions that threaten to overwhelm us in the wormhole on the way to the OtherSide.

Leaders sense that they can't thrive in the wormhole without a keen awareness of the God of Jesus. The Holy Spirit is that presence. Only the chaotic, unpredictable, spontaneous presence of the Spirit can give balance in the wormhole. Every image of the Spirit describes how the Spirit gives balance to the chaos. The very presence of the Spirit is experienced by its motion, its capacity to flow.

- wings of a dove
- flames of fire
- moving breath
- unpredictable wind
- annointing oil
- new wine

Jesus lives and breathes in our lives as the Spirit of God.[9]

In turbulent times such as the one we are in, people are prone to speak about the need for "anchors." Anchors are deadly metaphors in the wormhole. Anchors hold us in place and stifle our imagination. If you have ever anchored a boat, you know that while anchored you don't go with the flow. You are stationary, always looking off the stern of the boat, which means you are looking backward, watching the flow pass you by. Sounds like too many church leaders I know. Being "in the flow" is essential in the wormhole. The metaphors we need to concentrate on are:

"Jesus is the flow or stream of the Spirit ebbing in and out of our lives."

"Jesus is the lighthouse that guides us safely and swiftly through the jetties of life."

"Jesus is the Global Positioning System that steers us to our momentary destination."

Leaders who are attempting to imitate Jesus in the wormhole know that to stand still is to become irrelevant.[10] Leaders in the wormhole know that instead of praying for God to be present with them, the better prayer is to ask:

God, put us in the flow of what you are doing in this world; run over us with your presence. Help us be a part of your wondrous movements among us; do not let us see you come and go, and miss the wonder.

LEADERSHIP CLUE:

Leaders are constantly innovating "on the fly."

From Dave Travis of Leadership Network

Dave Travis of Leadership Network addresses some of the misperceptions people have about large, growing churches based on selections from key interviews of large-church pastors.

Misperception: All these churches have extensive planning systems where nothing ever goes wrong.

Not really. Sure, when the decision is for a new building or for relocation, they really take the time to think it through, but in general, I find these leaders to be in the "ready, aim, fire" category. These leaders are usually quick decision makers. They work on incredibly short time horizons for making changes. They make intuitive, instinctive calls that flow from their vision and just do it. This leads to frequent missteps. The difference between these leaders and others is that they are quick to admit mistakes and readjust the plan to make things work. Again, it is a bias toward action more than a bias toward reflection. These leaders and organizations make up for planning by being quick to readjust once something has started. Everything is in constant readjustment to align with what is working. In other words, these leaders and organizations tolerate failure. They try things and throw out what's not working.

Misperception: These superchurches have great preachers that draw a crowd.

Although there are some truly great preachers in the bunch, the majority are not. Don't get me wrong. They are excellent communicators. Instead of a classic, homiletical style, these pastors have a good sense of storytelling and, more importantly, life application. They are better communicators than preachers. They don't spend any more time in sermon preparation than an average pastor. They are "deep feeder" teachers. The benefit of listening to their teaching comes over time and repeated messages. There are few memorable messages from month to month but he consistency seeps into hearers' hearts and souls.

There is an advantage that these large-church leaders have over other pastors. Most have developed teaching/preaching teams that serve the congregation over the period of a year. Depending on the age of the senior pastor, the number of weekends where the lead pastor is preaching can be as low as thirty-two weeks a year. On average, I would say it is around forty to forty-two weekends. The other weekends are led by other teaching pastors and outside leaders or through special programs. This reduction of teaching load helps keep quality high. There is no reason why this cannot be done in smaller congregations as well.

Finally, these leaders have not only good oral communication skills but excellent interpersonal communication and relational gifts. It is not just their pulpit presence.

Misconception: These are really creative people.

No doubt, these churches tend to have some creative types, but in my opinion, the percentage is no more than in other churches. Instead, these churches are willing to borrow anyone's idea and put their own spin on it. When they see a good idea, they pounce on it. It doesn't matter if it's at another church, a business, or another nonprofit. They will jump all over it and adapt it to be unique to them. In contrast, I have been with churches that are very closed to ideas not invented at their place. In many of these congregations, outsiders are most unwelcome to help in finding new ways of carrying out their God-called mission.

Dave Travis works with Leadership Network and lives in Atlanta.

The wormhole does not stand still, nor does it progress linearly or evolutionarily. It spirals, twists, and turns, going forward and looking backward. But most of all it's moving fast. What appears to be up will be down and vice versa. It is much like trying to find one's way through the house of mirrors at the amusement park—a real head banger. Instead of the steep learning curve people speak of today, it is becoming more like a spiraling learning curve. About the time we think we've got it, the wormhole doubles back on us.[11] As Len Sweet is so fond of saying, it will be "ancient-future" and has a "double ring."[12]

The ability to constantly innovate "on the fly" will be essential for leaders in the wormhole. Innovating on the fly means living at the messy edge of chaos without becoming part of the chaos. Leaders who seek harmony and equilibrium will lead churches that stagnate and die. Like organisms adapting to the ecosystem's constant changes, leaders of effective churches constantly test the edges of church life. They don't just tolerate change; they build it into the fabric of their ministry and they equip others to come to grips with it.

Effective leaders today reside somewhere between absolute order and absolute chaos. The trick is to ride the wave of chaos to its crest without becoming engulfed by it. Instead of seeking order, leaders court the chaos. The worst thing a leader can do today is avoid the chaos of the moment for the order of the past. To do so signs one's death warrant as a leader and consigns the organization to death.

Five things are necessary for leaders to be able to innovate on the fly—imagination, a child-like curiosity, a willingness to repeatedly retool, an awareness that wild cards will come, and the ability to use symbols, metaphors, and art. Let's look at each one.

Leaders who innovate on the fly have strong imaginations. Imagination is the ability to clearly see what doesn't yet exist and to be able to articulate it so that others can also see it. Their ability to envision a preferred future defines the ride through the wormhole. The vision of a preferred future actually begins to mold today's actions and decisions almost as if it were self-fulfilling prophecy.

Imagination and innovation require a long list of scary things that are normally absent in most churches established prior to 1960:

- risk taking
- dreaming impossible dreams
- asking "why"
- being curious as to why things don't work or what it would take to make something work

- thinking outside the box or pushing the envelope
- doodling
- brainstorming
- playing "what if"
- letting the "inner child" out to play with dangerous ideas (more on this later)
- doing away with too many rules that clutter the church culture

Two important questions emerge at this point in our ride: *What happens in your church when someone has a new idea?* and *What systems does your church have in place that encourage the development of new ideas?* Innovation lies not so much in the creative genius of your leaders as in how much freedom they have to flex their spiritual wings and how much encouragement they get along the way. Most innovations come more from the result of unplanned, unauthorized, serendipitous actions than from some planned strategy to discover new ways of accomplishing the mission.[13]

Innovating on the fly will be easier if you:

- Go for the big, hairy, audacious innovations.
- Develop a permission-giving system.
- Never stifle an innovating moment—even if you're not sure if it is the thing to do.
- Move on to something else as soon as you get good at what you are doing.
- Gravitate toward the edges of your religious group.
- Listen to your instinct, not your critics.
- Do not obey nonexistent rules that may or may not have been required in the past.[14]

Christian Education can take a lesson from Disney's slogan for morning television, "Disney Playhouse, where learning begins with imagination."

Leaders who innovate on the fly have a childlike curiosity. My wife (Jan) and I have two mutts. Hershey is a creature of habit—always using the same path, every day, in the same way, to go to the same place. Hershey reminds me of church leaders who are bound by their habits—pastors who refuse to learn new paths to achieve old results. Watching them is like watching a rerun of a bad movie for the umpteenth time.

The other dog is Duke. Duke was chained up his first two years before we rescued him from a cruel neighbor. Now that he is free from his chains, he is curious about everything. Like a little child, every day is a new adventure. Nothing escapes his attention. He delights in forging new paths through the yard. Duke reminds me of the type of leader needed to navigate the wormhole.

Childlike leaders have several essential traits needed in times of great change. For one thing, they are used to things appearing larger than life. (Remember how large things used to look when you were a small child?) Great challenges excite them instead of intimidating them. The wormhole is just another adventure.

They also know what they want and are determined to get it. Like the young child sitting in the grocery basket at the checkout counter, staring at the candy, asking a parent repeatedly, "Can I have this? Can I, huh?" effective leaders are undaunted in their pursuit of God's vision. In my book *The Church Growth Handbook,* I called this trait the "two-year-old rule."[15]

Unafraid to ask *why,* they are filled with more questions than answers, making them very approachable leaders. They push the limits of most things and have no idea why something cannot be done. Failure is simply the prelude to learning something new. They have what Randall White, Phil Hodgson, and Stuart Crainer in their book *The Future of Leadership* call "a beginners mind."[16]

Childlike leaders are masters of trust. Trust is an essential element of leadership in an out of control world. Trust is the foundation of permission-giving leaders and networks, ongoing learning, team building, and a streamlined hierarchy. Childlike leaders look for and bring out the best in people. Without trust, transition seldom occurs.

Childlike leaders have limitless energy. The energy comes from an absolute certainty that they are in partnership with God. "For the sake of the gospel" energizes them and those around them. Seeing people give birth to God's gift inside of them brings out an energy that supercharges their lives.

The wormhole is so different and has so many possible outcomes that people with a bag of preconceived ideas will not do well. Throw out all of the sacred cows that clutter your life and experience the thrill and excitement of learning something new every day as you spiral from the world into which you were born into the world that is on the OtherSide of the wormhole.

Leaders who innovate on the fly repeatedly retool themselves. By retooling, I mean the total deconstruction of most of what one has learned about ministry and the reconstruction of a new set of Life Metaphors. These leaders constantly read from many fields outside religion, network with other effective pastors, and devour every learning opportunity.

Leaders who innovate on the fly expect wild cards to appear from time to time. Wild cards are out-of-the-norm things. Things that hit us broadside and cause us to have a headache. Wild cards are always a surprise, the last thing we would dream of happening or want to happen. Wild cards are low probabilities with very high impact on the future. A couple of recent wild cards are AIDS and the sudden rise of the World Wide Web.

Because of the wormhole and the inevitable chaos it will spawn, wild cards will come faster and be wilder than ever before. It is therefore imperative that leaders going through the wormhole expect the unexpected and are able to recognize the first signs of such events.

Three questions might help with wild cards: What are the most important wild cards for me, my organization, and my customer? How can I anticipate and appreciate these things? What can I do about my wild cards?

On your way through the wormhole, you will do well to interpret the ride in light of the following words: *incomplete, journey, complex, community, story, deconstructing,* and *both/and.*

Leaders who innovate on the fly make great use of symbols, metaphors, visuals, poetry, and art. If leaders can say it all with words, they have missed the point. Just as in the first century, in the wormhole we will have to share the gospel without the aid of print. The art of story and picture will emerge as primary forms of communication.

Tomorrow's churches won't be built on great oratory. Symbols, images, and art are replacing the talking-head sermon. One of the assumptions made in this book is that the wormhole is much like the first century of Christian history. Instead of passing on information through the use of books, people relied on oral tradition, symbols, and art. One of the most important functions of religious art through the centuries has been to bring to life the story of Jesus to people who could not read or who did not have access to a Bible.[17]

As we enter the wormhole, pictures, computer generated graphics, and electronic ink are occupying more of our time. We are becoming a Windows or perhaps a Linux world, leaving DOS farther and farther behind. Three points and a poem won't work anymore. People don't fill in the blanks during worship. If people can't join the message at any place and get the point, it won't preach on the OtherSide.

Sequential logic no longer communicates. The worst thing one can do in public speaking is to tell people what you're going to tell them, then tell them, then tell them what you told them. People will not be convinced and brought to faith as much through logic as through the heart and personal experience.

Leaders dream and daydream. In their minds and hearts they go places most of us have never thought of, and they take us with them. They spin grand tales of a "land with milk and honey" and people listen because they hunger for an ecstatic experience rather than for hearing mere words.

Symbols, metaphors, and visuals are power. They determine and convey how we feel and think. They are the stuff of who we are.[18] Symbols point to a reality that exists behind and beyond the symbol. Symbols allow us to direct our attention to something without pinning it down. Symbols leave the mystery to be contemplated instead of a fact to be explained and contained.

Metaphors are well suited for life in the wormhole since they never actually claim to describe reality as it really is. Instead, metaphors have an odd and ill-fitting way of suggesting many possible aspects of the reality to which they refer. Metaphors help us see in 3-D instead of one dimension. The point of metaphor is to evoke more than one way of perceiving a reality, to see the both/and instead of the either/or that so plagues the modern world.

Metaphors allow us to visualize something from a variety of different angles and perspectives. "Life is a game" or "the world is a stage." We can see old realities yet see them differently. We can stretch our imaginations and open new vistas of thought. Metaphors extend our insights and suggest new forms of action on our part, helping to make us more flexible. Metaphors are powerful tools of communication. They keep our minds pliable and our imaginations on fire. Metaphors are also paradoxical, allowing us to see more than one dimension of an idea. They can also distort the truth. We all know Jesus was not real bread, but we also know he is the sustenance of our lives.

Jesus was a master of metaphors. Most of us have experienced the power of the "I am" passages in the Gospel of John. "I am the bread of life" (6:35). "I am the gate" (10:9). "I am the good shepherd" (10:11). "I am the way" (14:6). "I am the vine, you are the branches" (15:5). Jesus used a variety of metaphors to describe himself and his relationship to God and to us so that we could have many ways of understanding the depth of who he is and what he should mean in our lives.

Leaders must be innovating in uncertain times. They must be able to see and communicate new ways to achieve old results. Symbols, metaphors, and visuals are a powerful way of seeing old experiences in the light of a new day.

Change Is No Longer the Issue

Ours is a time likened only to a handful of previous times in recorded history. I am referring to such discoveries as fire, the wheel, writing, the printing press, and engine-driven devices.[19] Each discovery has altered our view of ourselves and the world around us. We are living in such a time now.

Change is not the issue: radical discontinuity is the issue. Everything is in flux, moving from genesis to death and vice versa. Everything is being uprooted before our eyes. We are literally moving from one world to another.

This book took longer to write than any of my other books. I think that's because leadership issues kept changing as fast as I wrote about them. About the time I thought I had a leadership principle figured out, it changed. As soon as I realized there are no principles, no rules, just some clues, I was able to finish the book.

The following lists give some indication of the world on the OtherSide of the wormhole.

This Side of the Wormhole	The OtherSide of the Wormhole
Matter Only	Mind, Spirit, and Matter
Greek	Hebrew
West	East
Command and Control Models	Permission Giving
Evangelism Explosion	Relational Evangelism
Competence	Trustworthiness/ Authenticity
Position	Influence/Relationship
Committees	Teams
Making Disciples	Disciples Who Make Disciples
Program	Missions

Denominational Missions	Local Church Missions
Denominational Emphasis	Affinity Emphasis
Addition	Multiplication
Established Churches	New World Churches
United States Church Leadership	Third World Leadership
Customer Service	Customer Experience
People as Targets	People as Resources
Staff as Overhead	Staff as Resources
Learn Then Do	Learn While Doing
Education	Edutainment
Mostly Anglo Leadership	Mostly Ethnic Leadership
Work in the Church	Work in the Community
Pledging Is Out	Strategic Givers Are In
Job Descriptions	Adding Value
Budgets	Various Missions
Competition	Cooperation
Experts	Amateurs
Either/Or	Both/And
Modern Age/Christendom	Pre-Christian
Baptized Before Eighteen	Baptized After Eighteen
Grew Up in Church	Grew Up Outside of Church
Rows and Lines	Circles

I am far from the only one saying that change is no longer the issue. Leonard Sweet and William Bridges write about the difference between change and transition. Bridges says transition is when one learns how to cope with change.[20] Sweet takes it one step further and says that transition is when change changes from incremental to exponential. In *SoulTsunami,* Sweet writes, "Transition is supersonic change at the edge of chaos that phases from incremental to exponential."[21]

I want to carry this thought even further. "Supersonic change at the edge of chaos" isn't quite what I'm trying to say. That still leaves us on this side of the chaos. We are beginning even now to move past the edge of chaos into a world that absolutely no one can comprehend at this point. We are in the midst (not the beginning) of something so profound that when it's all over, those of us left standing will look upon the twentieth century as it looked upon the Dark Ages. That world is the subject of the next chapter.

Journal Entries and Other Painfully Wonderful Experiences to Make You Feel and Think and Enter the Wormhole

1. Describe the wormhole in your own words.

2. Describe where you are in relation to the wormhole—at the opening, in the middle, or on the OtherSide? How does where you are make you feel? Record your feelings. You may need them later.

3. How do you think the wormhole will affect you? Do you like what it is doing to you? Do you want to change the results?

4. What changes do you think you must make to help your church move through the wormhole? Keep these and later compare them to how you feel toward the end of the book.

5. Look back at most of your leadership. Have you transformed more lives than you have befriended or cared for?

6. Do you believe that you can be any kind of leader you choose to be? If not, what are your reasons?

7. If you are a member of a small group studying this book, discuss the answers to these questions.

8. Can you share the story of Jesus without words or print? Watch the movie *Amistad*. A wonderful picture of the world to come can be seen in the segment in which one slave leads another slave to faith in Jesus Christ with nothing more than the pictures in the Bible. Since neither slave was literate, the Christian

slave led the nonbelieving slave to Christ by simply moving him through the pictures in the family Bible.

9. A study of the following biblical material will give you a feel for some of the literature that was forged during the Exile: the book of Lamentations, Isaiah 40–55, Jeremiah, and Hebrews 11.

10. For a thorough comparing of today to the Exile, read Walter Brueggemann's book *Cadences of Home* (Louisville: Westminster John Knox Press, 1997).

11. Look at the list of **What Was** and **What Is** on page 39 and circle the words that best describe your view of reality. Put an X by those you do not understand. If you don't understand these by the end of the book, go to our website and record your question at **www.easumbandy.com/OtherSide** and see what happens.

Portal 3

The Death of Two Kissing Cousins

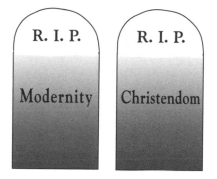

The common and widespread view is that the modern West, with its modern science, has more or less in one massive step, massively rejected soul and spirit, God and Goddess, sacred Nature and immortal soul—and left us with a modern wasteland.

—Ken Wilber

IMAGINE ALL THE VALUES BY WHICH YOU WERE REARED disappearing into a wormhole never again to be seen in your lifetime. That is the world of the wormhole.

As we move through the wormhole, we are witnessing the death of two kissing cousins—the *Modern Age* and *Christendom.*

Consider the Death of the Modern Age

The last five hundred years are known as the Modern Age (Modernity).[1] Modernity was shaped by such people as Descartes, van Gogh, Galileo, Newton, Marx, Freud, and Gutenberg, and included both the Renaissance and the Enlightenment.

During this period of time, science and religion were locked in what Ken Wilbur calls a "deadly dance" to see who was king.[2] Battles raged between science and religion in an attempt either to defeat one or the other or to bring them in line with each other. Ultimately, science finished the dance and won the prize. Physical matter, rather than the holistic approach of every premodern culture, became the fundamental building block. If something wasn't scientifically observable, it didn't exist. Matter existed; spirit didn't. Human consciousness was simply the conjunction of a combination of genes and never was the cause of change itself. Paranormal phenomena were dismissed as science fiction. Modernity took the soul and mystery out of the Western view of the cosmos, and life became one-dimensional, having no inner depth.

On the OtherSide of the wormhole, matter and spirit are kissing cousins instead of enemies. The wormhole is challenging the dominance of the purely objective, scientific worldview.[3] An interest in transcendence and the supernatural is returning. Belief in spiritualism is on the rise. We are moving closer to the cosmic worldview of reality prior to the Modernity in which mind, spirit, and matter were viewed as different parts of the whole. Spiritualism, faith healing, astrology, belief in UFOs, reincarnation, and fortune-telling are all experiencing a resurgence in interest.[4]

The foundations of Modernity are crumbling, and with it the modern understanding of the word "church." The discoveries of quantum mechanics shattered the closed mind of the scientific community by proving that there is no such thing as a fixed, totally certain body of knowledge. Something seems always to be unknown, always beyond the grasp of scientists. Things may not always be as they appear.[5] More and more scientists are concluding that the only way to make sense out of the logic of the universe is to believe in a divine hand in creation. More scientists are realizing that there is a complex interaction of the emotional and spiritual world with the world of physical matter as seen in the recent studies on how prayer affects the outcome of surgery. Every aspect of life is slowly acknowledging that something profound is happening at this moment in history.[6]

Unlike Modernity, life in the wormhole is multidimensional. Think of it as 3-D. If you've ever been to one of those movies where you have to wear those dumb glasses in order to see the 3-D effect, you know that the things in the movie seem to jump out of the picture and get "in your face." That's life in the wormhole. It's up-front, in-your-face, multidimensional, open to interpretation, unpredictable, and above all an extremely exciting ride.

Consider the Death of Christendom

By Christendom, I mean a culture in which the laws, educational systems, business, commerce, and social interactions were unquestionably dominated by the church and Christian values. Christendom began when Constantine made Christianity the state religion. It is a culture that actively promotes the Christian faith and often disparages or even persecutes expressions of other faiths or no faith. Throughout Europe, North and South America, and much of Africa, Christendom has been the dominant culture and institutional religion for sixteen hundred years.

The power of Christendom is disappearing from the Western world. A high school student in the United States was forbidden to write an essay about Jesus Christ because the teacher did not consider Jesus a historical figure. United States athletes are routinely told that if they miss any kind of practice because of attending church they will be thrown off the team. Christendom and its ability to influence culture are going, going, gone.

In 1983, the church I pastored for twenty-four years began to notice that children in the second grade didn't know anything at all about Christianity—nothing about the Bible, the commandments, the Lord's Prayer—*nothing.* They were children of the wormhole who had grown up outside of the influence of Christianity. This was one of my first clues that at least our part of the world was going through something Protestants had never gone through before.

Two events drove the last two nails in the coffins of Modernity and Christendom. On October 31, 1992, Pope John Paul II lifted the edict of Inquisition of 1633 against Galileo for concluding that the earth revolved around the sun. Four years later, the Pope gave his blessing to Charles Darwin and his theory of evolution. With those two events, Modernity and Christendom drew their last breath.

In *Dancing with Dinosaurs,* I called the death of Christendom and the Modern Age a "crack in history."[7] All of yesterday's and today's values are disappearing into this crack never to be seen again. We are passing from a "what was world" to a "what is becoming" world. The subtitle of the book was *Ministry in a Hostile and Hurting World.* Although the book became a best-seller, I received a lot of flak over the subtitle. At the time (1995), it was inconceivable to many professional clergy and denominational bureaucrats in the United States that the emerging world could be as hostile to Christianity as I described it. However, around the world the subtitle had great appeal. Every year now in the United States the subtitle is getting clearer.

Children know dinosaurs can dance because they have danced with Barney. Do you believe they can?

The world on the OtherSide will not be recognizable. It is time we all came to grips with that reality and quit avoiding our responsibility and saying, "but we've never done it that way before."

How do you feel and think about the following?

The What Was Side	The What Is Emerging Side
Stable	Unstable
Predictable	Complex
Static	Fluid
Order	Chaos
Law	Permission
Linear	Random
Rational	Emotional
Dignity	Zaniness
Decency	Intoxication
Mainline	Deadline
Rigid	Adaptive
Structured	Bends/blends
The Brady Bunch	*Seinfeld*
Sesame Street	*Barney*
Customer service	Customer experience
Explanation	Experience
Gunsmoke	*The Practice*
Do you understand?	Have you experienced it?
Books	The Net
Volunteer	Servant

The Way Through the Wormhole

To make it through the wormhole, leaders must remember that we have never been this way before. The attitude and posture of the world in the wormhole has been experienced only once before by Christians, but never by Protestants (with the exception of groups like the Moravians, perhaps). With the collapse of Modernity and Christendom many parts of the world are back again in a time much like the first and second centuries A.D.

Tom Bandy and I described this world as pre-Christian in our book *Growing Spiritual Redwoods*.[8]

> Those thriving Christian organisms . . . have begun to draw a still more detailed map of the future. They have realized that the new era is more than "post-anything." *It is a pre-Christian world!* It is a world similar to the first century after Jesus. It is a world of technological change and population migration; a world of systemic injustice and apocalyptic longing; it is a world of excessive materialism and spiritual yearning; it is a world of deep anxiety and utter cynicism toward the religious institutions of the past.[9]

I choose not to use the term "postmodern" because it has so many different meanings. It says what the new world is not instead of what it is, and its use is even questioned by some highly respected authorities.[10] I prefer the term "pre-Christian" because life in the wormhole will be much like the first century of Christian history.[11] All of the rules were being rewritten by Christianity.[12] Christianity faced two primary challenges. In the first century, Christians had to learn how to communicate the God of Jesus Christ to pagans (people who believe in many gods). In the second century they had to learn how to combat heresy among Christian leaders, which gave rise to the beginning of formal doctrine.

Pre-Christians have grown up much differently from people in Christendom. Most pre-Christians have two distinguishing characteristics. They have grown up outside any influence of Christianity and have been mentored more by their peers than by their parents. As a result, they are intensely tolerant of a vast variety of viewpoints and gods.[13]

LEADERSHIP CLUE:

Leaders know how to share Jesus with pagans.

Early Christianity focused on learning how to communicate Jesus with pagans. Whereas communicating with pagans has always been the mission, something very different is underfoot today especially for Christians.

The "gods" in which pagans believe today go by different names than in the first century, but they are no less "gods." The list is legion: psychic 1-900 telephone lines, Wicca, astrology, success, happiness, popularity, money, sex, power, sacred spaces, and so forth. When Christians refer to God, pagans hear the word "god." Most nonbelievers today worship either many gods or a personalized combination of gods, a sort of "designer faith."

Designer faith is taking a little from this god and some from that god and a bit more from another, and rolling it all into a faith designed to be comfortable to the needs of the person. This explains why, when the United States pollsters ask people if they believe in God, understandably the vast majority answer affirmatively. In such a world, Christians can no longer assume that when they refer to "God" people are hearing what they are saying.

In such a world it isn't enough to simply talk about "God"—something both the Hebrews and the early church understood. They always defined which god they worshiped. For the Hebrews it was the God of Abraham, Issac, and Jacob. For the first- and second-century Christians it was the God of Jesus Christ.

To learn how to communicate in a pagan world Christians can take a lesson from the apostle Paul and the early apologists. Polytheism actually provided Paul an opening in which to spread the gospel. People then, just like today, were hungry for God. Many of the effective early Christians believed that all secular learning, and all pagan religions, were based on an imperfect perception of the truth that was fully revealed in Jesus. The pagan religions were attempts to feed that hunger just as the psychic 1-900 telephone lines are today. Various Christian theologians--including Paul when he was preaching at the Areopagus in Athens in Acts 17, and Justin Martyr, the famous apologist--argued that pagan philosophy and religion were a step in the right direction, but only a step. Only Jesus could get you all the way there. We must return to this understanding again without becoming bigots in the process.

H. Richard Niebuhr's *Radical Monotheism and Western Culture* points us in the right direction toward learning how to communicate in a pagan society. Niebuhr suggests that all humans must derive meaning from something in order to live. The operative word here is "something." For many people what that "something" is doesn't matter as long as it brings meaning to their lives.

The problem is that these "whatever suits us" designer gods, like all other gods, soon begin to demand our complete devotion and become jealous over any other gods who vie for our attention. The problem with gods is that they are temporary. Whatever it is to which we give allegiance soon begins to fail us, leaving us with the same empty hunger for meaning. Therefore, the gods in which we put our trust don't deserve our trust. We seem to know that intuitively.

This "failure of the gods" is the point at which the pre-Christian world resonates with the Christian message—if and only if it is radical. Watered-down faith won't cut it in the pre-Christian world. Pagans have experienced the slow death of the gods. They have experimented with you-name-it gods and found them wanting. They have even found friendship to fail to fill the void. They have tried almost everything and found it wanting. That is why they are on this desperate search for experience. All things, including their biological families, have proved to be charlatans.

This is where Jesus enters the picture. Jesus points us to the one source of meaning on which we can rely—the God who is the Alpha and Omega, the same yesterday, today, forever. The early Christians offered Jesus as an alternative to the fruitless quest for meaning found among the pagan religions. Today, we offer Jesus to pre-Christians searching for stability and something that lasts.

However, much of Christendom either no longer knows how to talk about Jesus or does not believe in doing so for fear of offending the "god of inclusiveness." To talk about Jesus as the "hope of the world" is offensive to many church leaders. Watered-down faith has nothing to offer in the place of the gods except another god who will also let us down. This is one of the reasons ecumenism is about dead. Any form of a compromised, watered-down, or even blended faith in a generic God does not communicate to people who hear "god" when we say "God." Therefore, the churches who are sharing about the God of Jesus Christ are communicating far better than those who are preaching about the love of a generic God.

Don't get me wrong. Being liberal or conservative or ecumenical is not the issue. The issue is not being willing to share with the world a radical expression of what it is about our relationship with Jesus that the world cannot live without knowing. In order to live such a faith, church leaders must have a firsthand, personal relationship with Jesus Christ that is expressed in radical obedience. An academic, catechistic, ethereal, armchair understanding of a detached god who loves us dearly does not communicate. Neither do pre-Christians want to hear about the "sweet, nice, antiseptic Jesus." They want to hear about and meet Jesus the savior who cared enough to die, the servant who suffered so that others might live.

The hallmark of pre-Christians is that to them all viewpoints are relative. You believe what you believe, and if it works for you, that's fine. Inclusion is at the core of their creed; the only thing they're closed-minded about is closed-mindedness. But the early Christians were notoriously closed-minded in an open-minded age. They knew that to commit yourself to God in Christ was to make difficult choices about what you would no longer believe and do. This is why the struggle with heresy mattered so much; there were boundaries you just couldn't cross.

Here, then, is the paradox when working with pre-Christians. Radical obedience is appealing to pre-Christians once they have experienced Jesus Christ, but not before. They are notorious in their rejection of judgmental attitudes and deeply distrustful of belief systems that tell someone who doesn't participate in the system that they are somehow "wrong," or even worse, "going to hell." The challenge of working with them, then, is to get them to experience the healing, liberating presence of God in Jesus Christ. The only way this happens is if Christians learn how to walk among pagans as Christians who imitate Jesus. This means we must spend more time with pagans than in church meetings. They must discover Jesus in us and see the connection to their life situation. What they so desperately seek cannot be imposed on them. It must be witnessed and experienced. Today, it is necessary to speak of the God of Jesus Christ.

The early church also focused on heresy within the ranks of Christianity. Christianity began as a relational, rather than propositional, religion. Everything depended on one's relationship with Jesus. The nature and person of this Jesus was so crucial to the early church that the early Christian writers, called *apologists,* spent much of their time arguing the case for Christianity against both paganism from outside and heresy from within the faith.[15] The early Christians found themselves locked into controversies between orthodoxy and heresy concerning the nature of the person of Jesus Christ. Who was this person? What did he do? What is his relationship to God? And what is our relationship to him?

For the early Christians, theology was Christology. Jesus Christ was everything. What made these debates so deadly was that much of what came to be identified as heresy was not anti-Christian but was often distinguished from Orthodoxy by shades of meaning, as in the case of Gnosticism.[16]

Today, as we enter the wormhole, Christians are faced with the same struggles. Why don't the things of this world fulfill us? Is there any ultimate meaning? Who is this Jesus? What did he actually do? What is our relationship to him? Relativism and the nature and person of Jesus Christ are again at the forefront of controversy within the faith. Is Jesus Christ the one and only way to God? Is he fully both divine and human?

The primary struggle of the pre-Christian age is to come to an understanding of what it is about our *relationship* with Jesus that the world cannot live without knowing. The trouble is that too many church leaders are not as comfortable talking about their relationship with Christ as they are debating whether or not Jesus is the only way to salvation. Yet that is all the pre-Christian age wants to know. What does Jesus mean to you? Tell me about your relationship with him. Why is the relationship so important? What difference has he made in your life? This also means we have to talk about a personal Jesus, not a theological Christ.

We are now at the heart of the wormhole and the essence of pre-Christian faith. It is all about our relationship with Jesus that makes us different. Jesus is all we have to offer the world. Nothing more or less. It is when someone comes to this awareness that he or she is ready to ride safely through the wormhole. Not a minute sooner.

Effective leaders know how to effectively weave their story and *the* story in such ways that they connect with others. The only one thing the church really has to offer people is the hope found in new life in Jesus Christ. It is not enough to have a propositional assent to a belief in Jesus Christ. Such a faith is one of the reasons 85 percent of our churches are in trouble. Educated and informed pastors and laypeople can talk about Jesus Christ but they find it impossible to share with others their experience with him.[17]

We are living in a time of wild-eyed experiential spirituality. People are testing new forms of faith. Everything is relative. Now, as in the first four centuries A.D., the biggest challenge to Christianity is the threat from within the faith. Heresy in and out of the church runs rampant. Most church members are now a combination of heretic and biblical illiterate. In such a world, leaders have to be able to offer a solid, life-claiming theology that is grounded in Jesus Christ. Because the primary emphasis today is on our *relationship* with Jesus, and the world is virtually without rules, it is necessary to raise a new group of apologists who will produce a pre-Christian apologetic for our time.[18] Are you the one to do this?

Wormhole Nodes

Speed
Networks
Flexibility
Community
Relationships
Hope

It's Time to Step into the Wormhole

In case you haven't figured it out yet, the world has already pushed you into the wormhole. Realizing what you've stepped into is the shocker. You've entered a twilight zone in 3-D living color. The wormhole is deconstructing everything—except our faith in Jesus Christ. Those church officials who deny the centrality of Jesus Christ or who attempt to play down his central role, devaluing either the historical Jesus or the Christ of faith, will find themselves without a reference point and will be rendered useless as guides through the wormhole. On this point there can be no quarter given whatsoever.

In the wormhole, Jesus is our field guide. He is all we can hold on to. Nothing else will do, not denomination, not family, not nation, not even our doctrine, for the very thing we insist on preserving might be the one sacred cow standing between us and what God is doing in the wormhole.

Nothing gives leaders more credibility than the character and competency arising from a relationship with Jesus Christ—not credentials, profession, job title, level of responsibility, or income. In the wormhole, the source of respect for leadership and authority is shifting from academic and credential-based to an emphasis on character, gifts, and demonstrated competence. A leader's ability to lead other leaders now rests on an authentic relationship with God and one's inner character. To base one's identity or authority on anything else will be fatal to one's leadership ability.

As we go through the wormhole, our heads and hearts may spin and pound. Our adrenalin may pump. But here's a word of hope. We have an equalizer, a stabilizing force, as we spiral toward the OtherSide.

Jesus Christ is the same yesterday and today and forever. (Hebrews 13:8)

Grab hold of him and never, never let him go and you'll make it through to the OtherSide in one piece!

Journal Entries and Other Painfully Wonderful Experiences to Make You Feel and Think and Enter the Wormhole

1. Which one of your values is tested most by the changes occurring all around you? Are any new values emerging that you did not have a few years ago? What caused these new values to appear in your life?

2. Circle the words on page 71 with which you resonate the most.

3. Describe in your own words the difference between Christianity and Christendom.

4. When do you think Christendom actually ended? Is it still somewhat alive in your community? If so, describe it. If not, what most about it do you miss? Describe the difference between Christianity and Christendom to an alien.

5. Children are fascinated with dinosaurs and, of course, Barney. To have some fun with your child or children go to **www.barneyonline.com** and see what you can do together. Also see **www.weblog2000.com/ barneyskidpage**.

6. If a person who had never been to church in his or her life and had never been under the influence of Christendom became a Christian and was asked to design a worship service, do you think it would look anything at all like what a person who grew up in church would design, even if they were the same age? What do you think the non-Christian would come up with?

7. To get a feel for how pervasive such things as Wicca or astrology are, go to any search engine and see how many sites are devoted to spirituality of all kinds. *Alta Vista* or *dogpile* will yield the most results. Just type in "spirituality."

8. H. Richard Niebuhr on several occasions showed that any major change in society leads to the emergence of new Protestant denominations. Which ones are you seeing being started around you? How many possibilities of new denominations have you seen?

9. Write down the important aspects of your relationship with Jesus. Which ones mean the most to you? Which ones do you see others needing?

10. For the more courageous readers, share these thoughts about Jesus with a loved one, friend, or neighbor.

11. Look back at the list of **What Was** and **What Is** and circle the terms that best describe your view of reality. Put an X by those you do not understand. If you do not understand those by the end of the book, go to our website and record your questions in the appropriate spot at **www.easumbandy.com/OtherSide**. You will get a response from me.

12. To find out more about the writings of the first few centuries go to **www.iclnet.org/pub/resources/christian-history.html#fathers**. Also, read one or two of the second-century Patristic writings. What does it tell you about some of the major concerns of Christianity prior to Christendom?

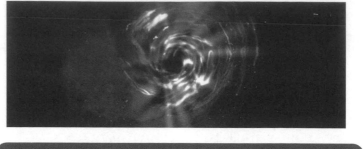

Portal 4

The Mother Life Metaphor

The quantum world teaches that there are no pre-fixed describable destinations. There are, instead, potentials that will form into real ideas, depending on who the discoverer is and what she is interested in discovering. Only by venturing into the unknown do we enable new ideas to take shape, and those shapes are different for each voyage.

—Margaret Wheatley

The kingdom of God is as if someone would scatter seed on the ground, and would sleep and rise night and day, and the seed would sprout and grow, he does not know how. The earth produces of itself, first the stalk, then the head, then the full grain in the head. But when the grain is ripe, at once he goes in with his sickle, because the harvest has come.

—Mark 4:26-29

I MAGINE A CHURCH SO ENVIRONMENTALLY RICH THAT everyone under its influence is encouraged to reach their God-given potential. That's the kind of church birthed by leaders on the OtherSide.

However, most traditional churches function like mindless machines. Many church leaders act as if "church" were a machine to be maintained rather than an organism to be nurtured. They do so because the primary Life Metaphor of the modern world has been that of a machine.

As we pass through the wormhole to the OtherSide, the machine Life Metaphor is blurring into the organic Life Metaphor. On the OtherSide, the organic Life Metaphor will prevail as surely as the machine Life Metaphor has prevailed in Modernity.

An organic view of life is the mother of all metaphors on the OtherSide. When this metaphor changes, all metaphors will change. The following chart gives an overview of this blurring.

Machine Life Metaphor	Organic Metaphor
Addition	Multiplication
Quick Fix	Long-Term Nurture
Restructure	DNA
Inanimate	Living
Predictable	Unpredictable
Needs Oil	Needs to Grow
Precision	Fractal
Replace a Part	Graft or Replant
All Models the Same	All Organisms Different
Works Only One Way	Grows in Many Ways
Each Part Distinct and Separate	Each Cell Contains the DNA
Linear Logic	Fuzzy Logic
Reengineering	Planting
Restructuring	Equipping
Downsizing	Pruning
Replacement Parts	Grafting
One Size Fits All	Diversity

The shift from the machine to the organic Life Metaphor is so pervasive that it is blurring all of our unconscious assumptions, rules, and prejudices that form the basis of how we feel, think, and act about life within and on the OtherSide of the wormhole. Leaders who understand "church" as a living organism feel and think much differently about the way they give leadership than those who consider their church to be a machine. These leaders are not mechanics who fix, or managers who maintain things. They are gardeners who grow people and plant churches.

The Machine Life Metaphor

Descartes, sometimes called the founder of modern philosophy (seventeenth century), taught that all phenomena, animate and inanimate, could be explained solely by mechanistic physics—that is, by the motions and collisions of bodies. Modernity separated soul from body and cleared the way for the mechanization of the church and the human soul. Over the next three centuries, Western civilization often referred to the universe as a grand old clock that could be dissected and reengineered to do whatever we wanted it to do. When it broke, we actually thought we could fix it. In time, even the human body was likened to a wondrous machine. The machine metaphor dominated the thinking of Modernity.

With such a Life Metaphor all one has to do to make a better church is focus on creating a better functioning machine—a little oil here or a new part there does the trick. Reengineer! Restructure! Downsize!

Much of the twentieth century's attitude toward "church" stems from the legacy of Frederick Taylor (1856–1915), the father of scientific management, and Henry Ford, the developer of the modern-day assembly line.

Taylor is known for his passion for efficiency. One of Taylor's main goals in life was the elimination of human decision making and creative thought because it was not the most efficient way to accomplish precision-like productivity. Taylorism robbed the workplace of any emotion and personal fulfillment. Duty replaced fulfillment. In such an environment, enjoyment should not be expected in the workplace or in the church.[1]

In a similar fashion, Henry Ford's passion for the assembly line took the soul out of work. People weren't expected to think or make decisions. They were good for putting the right part in the right hole at the right time—something any dumb machine could do. Henry Ford once complained that when he wanted to hire a pair of hands, he had to hire a whole person. Both Taylor and Ford left the twentieth century with a mechanistic, compartmentalized approach to life that will not work on the OtherSide.[2]

As a result, the machine became the great archetype. Our bodies were seen as the ultimate machine; our organizations had parts and specification that insured they gave a well-oiled performance. Even scientists began to talk about the universe as a machine.

Most established churches are ruled by people who grew up under the influence of Taylor and Ford. Churches are thought of as institutions, to be run by modern management principles. Pastors are spoken of as CEOs.[3] Seldom are laity thought of as God's servants in ministry. "Church work" has replaced mission and ministry.

Examples of the domination of the machine metaphor in established churches are abundant. Church leaders become so fired up over some new concept they have learned that they try to implement it without considering its implications for the rest of the body. Leaders think that if they could raise more money all their problems would vanish. Church leaders look for programs they can make work at their churches. They want to learn new, quick tricks that will change their churches in a few months. Finance committees approach church budgets in line-item fashion, separate and apart from any clear relationship to one another or the mission of the church. Pastors debate whether the offering should be placed before or after the service. When faced with a crisis, church leaders seldom ask what is the best decision for the long term. When faced with a financial crisis, church leaders cut their budget without any consideration of future consequences, or they have another fund-raiser without asking why they are running out of money. Most job descriptions treat paid staff as robots that perform specific duties and keep them in tiny little boxes. Seldom do I see a church where all the bits and pieces are tied together in a cohesive systems approach. Most churches treat people as if one size fits all, and they seldom have processes in place to address the needs of people where they are at the moment. In most churches everything is generic—generic stewardship drives, job descriptions, curriculum, ministries, staff configurations, and so forth. Worship services are a combination of many pieces, each standing by itself, often not having anything to do with the other pieces of the service. The more denominations decline, the larger the rule book becomes.

These leaders are usually well-meaning people who are very loyal to their denomination or church. The problem is that they view the church as a machine that can be fixed, instead of an organism that has to be nurtured.

Machines don't grow. The machine Life Metaphor robs people of their desire to grow. Any time a system is centralized and standardized, some small group makes a decision about how much people are allowed to think on their own. Learning and authority are centralized and transmitted along a clear chain of command. Harmony is more important than creativity. The last thing the church wants is individual expression.

Machines don't have passion. The machine Life Metaphor drains the soul, passion, and heart out of an institution, leaving it cold, predictable, calculating, and sterile. Board meetings become business sessions. Prayer becomes perfunctory. Following procedure and reading the minutes is more important than listening to the still small voice.

Machines require conformity and compliance. The more mechanical the Life Metaphor, the more controlling the environment. The last thing one wants a machine to do is get out of control. Thus, leaders seek to control everything in the church.

Members in machine-oriented churches see lay ministries as ways to fulfill a duty to the church rather than one of the major avenues for finding personal fulfillment. They often refer to their efforts as "church work" from which they look forward to retiring.

Machines aren't creative. The more mechanical the Life Metaphor, the less tolerant church leaders are of innovation. Creativity is never encouraged. Like a machine, people are expected to perform in a predictable manner—thus the life-threatening phrase "We've always done it that way."

Machines are inflexible. The machine Life Metaphor takes away the flexibility of the organization. Most machines are designed to do one thing at a time.

The problem with the machine Life Metaphor is that not one of us experiences life as a machine, and neither does the "church." Life is full of heartache and joy. Life has passion, not parts. It is unpredictable, full of surprises. Life can't be fixed or reengineered; it must be *grown.*

Thank God the metaphor is changing as we move through the wormhole.

The Organic Life Metaphor

The organic Life Metaphor feels and thinks of "church" as a living, breathing soul—an organism that requires regular and ongoing nurturing, not restructuring; gardeners, not administrators or CEOs. Health, growth, and reproduction are the archetypal metaphors. The only way to measure the health of an organism is by asking, "Is it growing and reproducing?"

Seed, growth, and flower describe the organic process in a plant. Which comes first, seeds or flowers? Sperm, growth, and adult describe the organic process in a human. Which comes first, the sperm or the adult? What we do know is that without growth neither is possible. Growth is essential for seeds to bloom into flowers and children to mature into adults.

Organic life grows effortlessly and naturally and does not have to work at growing. Deepak Chopra says, "Grass doesn't try to grow, it just grows. Fish don't try to swim, they just swim."[4] In her delightful book *A Simpler Way,* Margaret Wheatley says that life exists to organize around its DNA.[5]

When churches know their DNA and individuals use their genes to enhance the DNA, growth *just happens.* Just like grass grows and fish swim, organic churches grow. This truth is difficult for modernists to hear, much less comprehend, because they are used to thinking of the church as a machine. Machines have to be told what to do and where to do it, but organisms are designed to grow by their DNA.

The human spirit was made to explore and soar, not to be regulated and intimidated. People are created to be free, not controlled; to experiment and make mistakes, not to be oiled and greased; to test their creative genes in order to reach their God-given potential, not to perform like machines or robots. The organic Life Metaphor provides an atmosphere in which such potential can be explored and often reached.

Organisms are always in relationship with the environment around them. Like machines, organic systems form a distinctive differentiation from the environment, but unlike machines, they also maintain a constant relationship with the environment. Instead of insisting on a controlled environment, like most machines, organisms know that their survival and growth depends on their interconnectedness to the world around them, and they learn to adapt ahead of the changing environment. Nothing lives in isolation in the organic world. Any change in any part of the environment eventually affects every other part. Compartmentalization is not even conceivable.

Organisms change only to achieve what they were created to do. They read the environment and they decide what they have to do to communicate with it in such a way that they play a productive part in their surroundings.

Passing through the wormhole requires constant adaptation to the swirling environment. Change is part of life. Organisms are in constant flux. The human body is constantly sloughing off and reproducing its cellular structure. To refuse to change means to cease to exist. Those with an organic Life Metaphor feel and think about "church" as a fluid system that is dying, growing, dying, and renewing all at once.

DNA is what defines a species and makes it distinct. Every cell in the body—every person in the church—has the same DNA, and every cell contains all the DNA for the entire person. However, DNA is designed in such a way that it makes everything in the world individualized. A female X chromosome and a male Y chromosome go through a process called *meiosis,* which mixes up the genes in each individual and at the same time carries characteristics of the parent to the offspring.[6] Each cell in the person's body contains the entire DNA of the person. DNA also tells each cell what body function it is to specialize in.

The church is an organism with DNA.[7] The DNA defines who we are without making us all exactly the same. It allows each part of the Body of Christ to be different while focusing on the same God-given mission. It provides the parameters that we can empower one another to work within, resulting in a common vision being realized through our diversity. We can focus on what we have in common without giving up our uniqueness.

Unlike physical human DNA that can't be changed (at least not yet), spiritual DNA can be changed. It is called the "new birth" (John 3:3). In Christ, people become new creatures and the church a new creation, a holy priesthood. Our core identity changes; our DNA is altered.

The DNA of any legitimate Christian endeavor is to make disciples of Jesus Christ. As such, leaders on the OtherSide believe in the re-creative power of Jesus Christ, just as the very first disciples did. This belief is under attack within the central core of much of established/mainline Protestantism. Many people look for salvation in social justice, in gaining more knowledge, eating healthy foods, getting back to nature, getting in touch with their inner selves, or through conversation with a psychotherapist, journaling, dream interpretation, the psychic hotline, or through any combination of things all of which seem reasonable and worth trying but will never bring satisfaction unless they lead to Jesus, who is the source of salvation.

LEADERSHIP CLUE:

Leaders sense that the basic genetic code of the church is to make disciples of Jesus Christ, not to take care of people.

Jesus is recorded as saying, "Go therefore and make disciples of all nations, baptizing them in the name of the Father and of the Son, and of the Holy Spirit" (Matthew 28:19). "Go into all the world and proclaim the good news to the whole creation" (Mark 16:15). "You will be my witnesses in Jerusalem, in all Judea and in Samaria, and to the ends of the earth" (Acts 1:8*b*). You don't have to be a genius to understand these words.

Each statement was made at the very end of Jesus' life. The early church understood them to be his last will and testament. They are the heart and soul of Jesus and they tell us that the bottom line for any church is leaders who make disciples for Jesus Christ. Anyone who does not passionately believe this, is not giving spiritual leadership to a church no matter where it is located, how small or large it might be, or what age the members are. The church exists to bring people into a saving relationship with Jesus Christ. That is its biblical purpose. Period!

The primary reason so many churches are unhealthy and declining is because their leadership does not understand the biblical role of the church. This lack of understanding can be seen in the actions of denominational leaders. Almost every *dying* denomination is engaged in some form of study to determine the purpose of the church. Such action is nonsense. The Bible is crystal clear about the purpose of the church.

Education, information, and church membership have nothing to do with being a disciple. A disciple is one who intentionally seeks to emulate Jesus in everyday life. This means deliberately taking the cause of Christ (Luke 9:23-25), putting Jesus before self, family, and friends (Luke 14:25-35), committing to world evangelism (Matthew 9:36-38), loving others (John 13:34-35), bearing fruit (John 15:8), and abiding in and being obedient to Christ (John 5:7-17).

Too many churches function as if the primary role of the church is to minister to the sick and dying. Pastors spend much of their time driving from one hospital to another. Prayer concerns in churches are almost totally consumed by prayers for the sick. The next time you ask for prayer requests from a group of people, take note of the requests. Almost every prayer will be for the sick, the dying, those traveling, those celebrating a new birth, emotional health, or good news from the doctor. If you did this every Sunday for twelve months, most churches could count on one hand the number of times a prayer request was for someone's spiritual conversion. This is not what God intended for the church! The church is not a hospice where no one ever gets well. We are not in the health business. The church is a training ground for growing spiritual giants.

To make matters worse, many church leaders either assume that the decline of Protestantism is inevitable, or worse, they believe that the decline is part of God's plan as seen in the Old Testament "righteous remnant" theory. This belief in decline as being some part of God's great cause can be seen in the actions of local clergy. Many mainline/established church leaders are falling for this nonsense that God wants the church to decline. Some take a great deal of pride in it.

The DNA of the church is that it must bring as many people as possible into a redeeming relationship with Jesus. Therefore, the role of church leaders is not to take care of people. The role of church leaders is to provide opportunities for people to grow and blossom in their faith so that they can help others do the same.

Don't misunderstand me. Every church needs caregivers. However, that is not the primary role of a church no matter what the age of the members of the church. The primary role is to reach out to people with the gospel of Jesus Christ as described in Acts 6.

Many churches have confused DNA with genes. Our DNA is made up of various genes. Whereas the DNA of every Christian and church is to make disciples of Jesus Christ, our genes determine how we go about making disciples.[8] Having mistaken genes for DNA, it is easy for people to focus their attention on their own vision, values, and beliefs and avoid the basic DNA of the church. It is also possible for one church to have a kind of multiple-code syndrome—every pastor has imprinted various DNA strands into a church over the years. These DNAs don't fit together. Each is unique. Although many DNAs in and of themselves may actually be good codes, only one DNA can function within a body.

You can't have "competing" DNAs. Various groups and people cling to this DNA or that DNA, and so when a transformational leader comes along she or he finds it necessary to spend fifteen to twenty years imprinting *one* DNA that becomes common to the overwhelming majority. This is why every time such a pastoral change is made, some person or group is unintentially cast out of the body, because the new DNA violates their DNA. Church planters also experience a struggle with multiple codes when either they fail to develop the DNA of the new church before they begin to gather a core group, or their core group consists of disgruntled church members who want to hang on to various imprints from their previous church.

Organic churches imprint their DNA in every cell of the body. Their goal is for each cell of the body to replicate the DNA, providing them enough depth of leadership to thrive even in times of crisis. Because they have a common mission on which to draw, they are not blindsided when the rules of the game change. They are not limited to only what they can anticipate and plan.

Discovering the DNA

Leaders know that unleashing the DNA occurs when they assist other church leaders in discovering and articulating the DNA of the church.[9] Leaders serve as guides and interpreters of people's hopes and dreams. Leaders listen, discern, and then articulate the collective wisdom of the congregation.

Congregational DNA has been described many ways. Tom Bandy and I call it *mission, vision, value,* and *belief statements;*[10] Ken Blanchard uses *core values;*[11] Rick Warren says *the purpose-driven church;*[12] and Aubrey Malphurs interchanges *vision* for what Tom and I call *mission.*[13]

It doesn't matter how you describe the DNA as long as it describes the "Why," "How," and "What" of a particular congregation on which the leaders are willing to stake their claim. "Why does our church exist?" "How are we going to achieve this purpose?" "What are our values?"[14] The "How" and "What" can vary widely. The "Why" is more constant from church to church.[15]

"Why does our church exist?" is the *mission statement* of the church. The "Why" of every congregation is always some form of making disciples. This statement needs to be short enough for a six-year-old or a guest to remember.

"How are we going to achieve this?" is the *vision statement.* The vision statement tells how a particular church is going to carry out the mission statement. The vision will vary from church to church.

"What are our values?" is the *values statement.* The values statement sets the boundaries in which people are free to make decisions and live out their giftedness without asking for permission. Values set important boundaries that channel gifts in the right direction. Anything anyone wants to do that is within these boundaries and enhances the DNA can be attempted overnight without a church vote.

These statements guide all decisions and ministries so that there is need for few, if any, meetings to make decisions. When a meeting is required, discernment, rather than voting, is employed. Nominating committees are replaced by discernment and individual initiative in response to a clearly and often cast vision.[16] Self-organizing, self-governing, and self-destructing teams replace longstanding, nominated committees.[17] Once the DNA is discovered, everything the church does is measured by the DNA. No matter what comes along, the DNA is guarded and enhanced. Leaders are willing to drop anything or anyone that tries to destroy or does not enhance the core values. They're also willing to add anyone or anything that will enhance the DNA.

From Kurt Oheim

In our case, the DNA was determined before the church came together. It was the fruit of discipleship that occurred in my life (over a period of years) and in the lives of a few others. There was no retreat. No discussion. No calculations. The DNA was who I was and who we were (and are). In a way it was a "no brainer." Myself, my wife, and the fourteen other adults who started Pinnacle had the DNA within us already. Sure, we wrote it down, codified it, "cast it," but it was already woven into the fabric of our hearts, minds, souls, and bodies. Really. Once we were "assembled" together as a team of people with a common vision, Pinnacle took off at an amazing rate. I just say this as a form of my own amazement at the process and the rapid progress.

God-designed and spirit-guided elements that have been part of this experience are: (1) authenticity, (2) clarity of identity (DNA, core values, and so forth), (3) intense passion for our vision (helping people say yes

---

to God, and developing them), (4) a great leadership culture embodied in a team/small group developmental ethos, (5) minimal distractions over the past nineteen months, and (6) lucky (providential) timing and location. These have all come together to help us reach significantly more people each month. There's no bickering, no convincing, no long drawn-out committee meetings (we have no committees). We just do it. When we have elements that screw up on a given Sunday, we evaluate, regroup, and make the presentation of "the message" better the next week. I regularly meet with the various leaders one-on-one and as teams. (I eat a lot of lunches with these people and many times schedule two lunches a day—lots of salads.) I disciple them, encourage them, vision cast like crazy, give them breaks, celebrate them, and help them know that they are changing a very important part of God's world for eternity.

Kurt Oheim is pastor of Pinnacle Church, a new church in Amarillo, Texas (December 1998).

If the DNA is to become embedded in every person of the church, it must resonate deep down in the gut of the majority of the leadership; otherwise it becomes an ax wielded by a dictator. Nothing is worse than a plastic mission statement that does little more than hang on a wall or take up space on a shelf. I once asked a pastor if her church had a mission statement and she said, "Yes, but I'm not sure where it is." I asked her what it was and she said, "I don't remember." That church didn't have a mission statement, much less a *shared* mission statement.[18]

The primary role of the lead pastor is to be the keeper of the DNA and insure that it is embedded throughout the church. His or her role is to constantly reinforce the mission (DNA) of their particular church. It seems as if people are prone to forget their mission every seven to twenty-one days.[19] The primary reason vision casting seldom works is because the vision caster forgets to focus on casting and recasting the vision over and over. The effective leader never misses an opportunity to reinforce the DNA—every sermon, conversation, article, meeting, Bible study, book, paper, and retreat.

It should become clear to everyone that the intention is for these statements to become the actual leadership of the church instead of the board or council or deacon or session or whatever. This is a huge shift that must be understood by everyone. Every decision will be measured by these statements. "If we do this, will it carry out the essence of these statements?"

The clearer everyone is at this point, the easier the ride will be through the wormhole to a permission-giving, values-driven church. The question of who decides is greatly reduced. The statements decide and anyone is free to interpret them and act upon them (of course, common sense, laced with faith, must abound). When someone does something that violates the spirit of the statements, they are held accountable by whatever group the congregation sets aside to do this.[20]

From my work with four major churches in the United States, I have learned the following about what a church can anticipate as it seeks to discover its DNA.[21]

Leaders must lead other leaders. I'll never forget the small group that huddled with me in my home on my first Sunday evening as pastor of Colonial Hills Church. I discovered that night that these twelve people had the same understanding of the DNA of the church that I did, and they had had it for years. Astonished, I asked, "Why haven't you done anything about it?" not really expecting a response. But I got one. Almost in unison they said, "We didn't have a leader!" Each of these persons was already a leader in his or her own right. Still, they yearned for a leader of leaders.

There must be open and intimate dialogue between the leader and the pastor. Pastors must listen before they speak. They must trust the people enough to invite them into their lives. Listen to Mike Foss, pastor of Prince of

Peace Lutheran: "I shared with them what was in my heart and I listened intently to what was in theirs."[22]

The pastor must be willing to open him or herself to a considerable amount of self-evaluation, as well as evaluation from other leaders. The pastor must struggle with and face personal insecurities, doubts, and the need to control what happens. When asked what he would do differently, Michael Slaughter, pastor of Ginghamsburg United Methodist Church, said, "I would have given much more attention to my soul and that of my family."[23]

All paid and unpaid staff must be aligned with the results. They have to resonate with the mission, vision, and values of the church to remain on the staff. Most of the time, discovering DNA results in some staff deciding this is not the church in which they want to work. The most frequent casualty is the musician who is more concerned with teaching people to like good music than with using music to transform people.

High-expectation churches have much less trouble discovering their DNA than low-commitment churches. When people are held accountable in a system where there has been no accountability, DNA may feel like control at first. One lady said, "They changed the rules in the middle of the game." A staff person railed at me, "I didn't sign on for this." It is easy to see why some people might leave the church—painful, but not a big deal if our understanding of the church is organic. It matters more if people go to a church with their DNA than if they to go to a church because that is where they have always gone.

If confusion does occur, it is important for the key leaders to remain firm and not second-guess the process. In a short time, the dust will settle and people re-up with more energy and time commitment than ever before. In time, leaders won't have to think about decisions. Neither will they feel the need to get together and vote on everything new. New ministries will be cherished as much as the old. Like couples married for fifty years, they think and feel alike. Trust, not control, becomes the dominant culture. The day comes when saying yes to new ministries that enhance the DNA comes naturally.

Expect things to be out of control once you discover the DNA and equip the laity. The Spirit is always out of control. Be patient. Sit back and enjoy the ride. In time you'll see church members becoming disciples of Jesus, and ecstasy replacing anxiety or contentment. In time, leaders will savor new ideas and feelings and will become comfortable being out of control.

Leaders must be prepared for conflict. Conflict will occur while discovering the DNA, so some guerrilla/love tactics may help. Never take anything personally (this is often hardest for the spouse). More than anyone else, leaders set the climate and control the thermostat. If leaders heat up, so do others. The best way to keep one's cool is to keep in mind that no one is ever mad at you. They are mad at the fact that things are not what they used to be or things are not good at home or their lives just stink. Church is no longer the one place they can go where nothing is going to change. When confronted with stiff opposition from a handful of people, take a step back and pray, hit a golf ball, go for a walk, spend some intimate time with your spouse—whatever it takes to remain calm.

Often, in order for the church to discover its DNA, the pastor has to change before the congregation will change. As Pogo says, "We have met the enemy and it is us." Dick Wills, pastor of Christ United Methodist Church in Fort Lauderdale, Florida, tells how his trip to South Africa to get away from the debilitating task of going nowhere at his church resulted in a deeply moving experience in which he felt God share with him three core values that changed his life and the life of his congregation. When the congregation saw him living the life he was preaching, they began to sit up and listen. In time, they began to say, "We want what Dick has."[24]

Discovering DNA is a God thing. Being led by God is more important than being lead by rules, regulations, and policies. DNA is not another program or task to be completed, and it can't be legislated by a committee. DNA is who we are and what we're about as disciples of Jesus.

Replicating the DNA

Leaders know that unleashing the DNA occurs when they equip individuals to discover and use their own giftedness to enhance the DNA. We are now at the heart of what it means to lead in the wormhole and on the OtherSide. Leaders equip individuals to replicate the church's DNA through the use of their gifts. Their role is to create an environment in which people are encouraged to soar by discovering and living out their spiritual gifts. God gives each person special gifts to be used on behalf of the Body of Christ. Individuals discover their destiny when they are equipped to use their gifts on behalf of the Body of Christ.[25] Disciples are grown, not on preconceived organizational needs, but on the God-given giftedness of the individual.

However, in today's fast-paced world, it is not enough for leaders to do one-on-one evangelism. Multiplication is required on the OtherSide. Exponential growth, like on the day of Pentecost, is the goal. Leaders equip other leaders to grow disciples. They in turn are equipped to grow disciples.

Making disciples who make disciples is the heart of leadership. Leaders disciple other leaders instead of collecting followers. The DNA of every church is to grow more and more disciples of Jesus Christ. To eliminate this function is to cease to be a church and become a club with dues. Robert Greenleaf says:

> The best test, and difficult to administer, is: do those served grow as persons; do they while being served, become healthier, wiser, freer, more autonomous, more likely themselves to become servants?[26]

"Fractal" is the organic way to describe this type of leadership. Although fractals are a recent development of mathematics, the best way I know to explain them is to ask you to look at the leaf in Figure 4A. Notice the large vein running down the middle and the smaller veins branching out from the large vein. If you could magnify this leaf, you would see that each one of the smaller veins has even smaller veins branching out from it. Every part of the leaf bears an exact resemblance to the whole leaf. No matter how much you magnify the leaf, the pattern is repeated over and over. That's fractalling.[27]

Figure 4A

Fractalling is when leaders equip others to reproduce the DNA in every person and every part of the congregation. Leaders grow leaders who grow other leaders. This is the heart of leadership on the OtherSide.

Jesus didn't collect followers, he grew the leaders of tomorrow. He fractaled. He reproduced himself in a motley group of diverse individuals and then he sent them out to do the same. He didn't take care of people; he grew people. Fractalling takes serious our Lord's statement, "For where two or three are gathered in my name, I am there among them" (Matt. 18:20). That's what any successful leader will do in the wormhole.

The first time I read the New Testament, I was amazed at how little Jesus accomplished in his lifetime. If you look closely at the biblical record, you can't help noticing that Jesus didn't "do" that much. He often refused to help people. His primary goal was not to change the world but to equip a group of people who, in his absence, would change the world. His emphasis was not on what he would do but on what others would do because of him. He even said that we would do greater things than he did (John 14:12).

Thousands of people could be enriched by a redeeming relationship with Jesus if leaders only took the time to teach leaders the things they know. Perhaps you are a very good Sunday school teacher—then find and train four new people to do what you are doing. Perhaps you are very good at developing software that the church can use in worship—then train four other people to make this software. Fractalling, multiplying the church, depends on you training other people to do what you can do.

Imagine what this looks like in a congregation. Every leader mentors two or three potential leaders. Every person who joins the church starts a prayer group or Bible study or a support group for people they know who don't come to church. Every parent of teenagers receives training to understand how to reach out to the friends of her or his son or daughter. Every teacher is encouraged to find one or two other teachers who share his or her values, and begins a support network. Every office manager is taught how to deal with employee problems in ways that those being helped learn how to help others in similar situations. Every person who joins the church brings two or three people along. Leaders no longer come to church by themselves or just with their own family; instead, they bring friends, relatives, neighbors, or associates with them. Sunday school teachers and small group leaders do not teach or facilitate solo; they each have two or three people at their side whom they are training to go and do likewise. The person responsible for the visuals during worship doesn't just do the presentation, but has two or three people alongside learning how to do it. No longer do people say, "We'll let Raoul do that because he is an expert." Instead, they say, "Looks like you're ready to learn the next step—we'll get Raoul to teach you, then you can show Jan how to do it." In such a church, no one does anything of any value alone.

I experienced such a church in March of 1998 while working with the New Hope Christian Community Church in Honolulu.[28] They fractal every chance they get. Wayne Cordeiro is the keeper of the DNA. This new church has grown in less than four years to over 7,000 in worship (1999). Their four by four system is for the leaders who oversee any ministry in New Hope. They divide the span of care into groups of four. When a leader begins a ministry, a team of four is gathered around their gifts and passions, and the DNA is embedded in them. The leader breaks the new ministry into quadrants and each of the four leaders in training oversees one of the quadrants. If that ministry grows, each of the four leaders (overseeing one quadrant each) does the same thing that was done when they were recruited to be part of the team—they recruit four more people to work in their quadrant. This is called their second tier of leadership. If each of the four senior leaders builds his own team of four each, then twenty-one are in leadership of this new ministry. The more people who own the ministry the stronger it becomes. Then even as the first leader oversees and disciples his four, each of them in turn oversees and disciples another four. In this way, each is being discipled as well as discipling others. Everyone is always being trained and is training someone else. This church is living up to its mission, which is "to introduce people to Jesus Christ, to help them grow to be more like him, and then to reproduce the process in others."

Fractalling always results in a much more diverse group of leaders than the old nominate-and-elect practice. Authentic leaders grow other leaders based not on the gene pool of the mentoring leader but on the gene pool of the ones being mentored. Leaders do not impose on others how they must go about living out their leadership roles. The only thing that is necessary is that they embrace and embody the DNA. Because of the unique gene pool of each person, how each person carries out the DNA will be different. In other words, leadership is not about how one does something, but what one does with one's life—grow other leaders.

Jesus gathered a group of very diverse people. They came from different backgrounds, had different personalities, and performed their ministries much differently from one another. Aside from the basic DNA, to grow other Christian leaders, their genes made them different. The first Christian leaders mirrored the DNA of Jesus, but they were far from being his clones.

Fractals are sensory, messy, random, nonlinear, unpredictable, and fragmented. The more they're magnified the more unpredictable they become until finally their unpredictability becomes their stabilizing factor. See Figure 4A. Look at any leaf growing on a twig on a branch on a tree. It is nothing like a geometric pattern. That leaf grew in place because of a particular set of wind and light conditions. The twig grew a particular way because a caterpillar pooped on it one day. The branch grew at that angle because another branch was competing for the light. And every tree you look at, all over the world, is doing the same thing—growing uniquely in its own way. Endless multiplication of DNA is striving to get into the next generation and not a single scientist can predict exactly where the next year's growth will occur for the tree because no one knows where caterpillars or birds or snakes will poop next. Giving leadership to growing churches is like that. The more unpredictable a fractal becomes, the more predictable it becomes. Because of computers and fractals, chaos is no longer seen as the enemy of order and beauty, but as a precursor of the emergence of a new order.[29]

Job descriptions just get in the way of replicating the DNA due to the constantly changing nature of the environment. Job descriptions lead to inflexibility on the part of church staff as well as an "it's not my job" attitude. Leaders have to be flexible in the wormhole and go with the flow of the DNA. Leaders expect to have multiple learning opportunities on the same staff. Instead of keeping the same responsibilities year after year, leaders will regularly change responsibilities. Such types of promotions are called "horizontal promotions."[30]

Instead of a job description, all that is needed is the charge to find new people and equip them to use their spiritual gifts to enhance the mission of the church and to take responsibility for whatever ministry they choose. This is the "Jesus model."

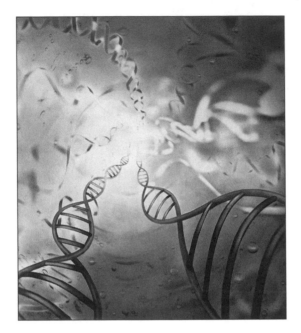

One of the learning experiences of the past few years is that replicating the DNA is more crucial than its actual discovery. Leaders spend the rest of their lives feeling, thinking, and living it out for the sake of the mission. They focus on it and align everything around it. John Wesley is a good example of alignment and focus. He had spent the first forty years of his life before he discovered his DNA, which was the class meetings.[31] He then spent the next forty years feeling, thinking, and living out that DNA without any change. We are seeing the same organic approach to emerging ministries all over the world.

In organic churches all leaders replicate the DNA throughout the church in every cell and at every level. The primary paradigm shift today in the area of church staff is the movement away from staff doing ministry to staff equipping others to do ministry. Instead of going to work thinking about what one must do, the staff goes to work dreaming about who they might meet, transform, and mentor. Instead of trying to get ministry done or a task performed, staff look for new people to mentor, equip, and send out into ministry. The shift is from doing to finding.

All leaders must ask not "What must I do today?" but "Who will I mentor today?" Not "What is my job?" but "Who will I discover?" Not "How much can I do?" but "How many can I equip to equip others?" The discovering and equipping of this kind of paid and unpaid staff is the most important responsibility of the core leadership of a church.

Now you see an emerging picture of leadership on the OtherSide. Leaders grow people and lead leaders. The role of any effective lead pastor will be that of identifying, equipping, and placing other leaders into leadership so that they can go and do the same with others who will go and do the same with others, and so forth. The role of any effective leader is to embed the DNA throughout the church through the lives of those who are changed and grown by their contact with them. Leaders fractal.

Church leaders, throw away your "to do" lists and your job descriptions and be the DNA in every aspect of your lives.

A Personal Confession

Moving from a mechanical to an organic understanding of life will not be easy. So, let me confess again.

My Life Metaphors are challenged every time I use a public restroom. Until recently, most public restrooms were identified with big letters that spelled "men" or "women." Today, many of those same public restrooms are identified with a symbol instead of words.

I don't have any trouble whatsoever understanding the meaning of "men." It means that is the door I am supposed to enter. I grew up totally on this side of the wormhole. Words are my bag. I don't have to interpret the meaning of a familiar word. However, symbols aren't that simple—I have to interpret them. Is that a picture of a man or woman on the door? Is that symbol wearing pants or a skirt? I've walked into two women's restrooms because I did not correctly interpret those symbols!

At one time in my life I could read the Greek language fairly well, but as much as I tried, I never could think or feel in Greek. I could tell you what the words meant, but I couldn't process my thoughts in Greek nor did I ever completely feel as if I understood Greeks. That's how it is with many of us who were born into Modernity and Christendom and are now moving through the wormhole. It's not an easy journey.

As we go through the wormhole from mechanical to organic, our heads and hearts spin and pound. Our adrenaline pumps. So here's a word of grace. We have an equalizer, a stabilizing force, a balm in Gilead as we spiral toward the OtherSide.

> Jesus Christ is the same yesterday and today and forever. (Hebrews 13:8)

We are not alone in this journey. We have a traveling companion who will never abandon us or leave us for dead if the ride gets too rough. At every stage of the journey, we have the awareness that we are part of a journey and mission connected with Jesus. The journey is not something we began. It is something into which our love for God through Jesus Christ has drawn us. And this awareness of Jesus' presence, and his participation in the ride, constantly lifts us above the noise and the confusion of change and flux. It sustains us, fuels us, refreshes us, and guides us along the journey. Even in the wormhole, we are convinced that:

> Neither death, nor life, nor angels, nor rulers, nor things present, nor things to come, nor powers, nor height, nor depth, nor anything else in all creation, will be able to

separate us from the love of God in Christ Jesus our Lord. (Romans 8:38-39)

Grab hold of Jesus and never, never let him go, and you'll make it through to the OtherSide in one piece!

JOURNAL ENTRIES AND OTHER PAINFULLY WONDERFUL EXPERIENCES TO HELP YOU FEEL AND THINK AND EXPERIENCE THE MOTHER LIFE METAPHOR

1. In your own words describe the difference between machines and organisms. Which one best describes your view of reality and that of your church?

2. Which of the following two images portrays your church?

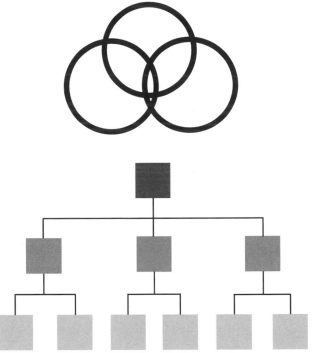

3. Why is it that 40 percent of the Fortune 500 companies that appeared on the 1979 list are not found on the list today? Any eye-openers here? A good study

book is James C. Collins and Jerry I. Porras, *Built to Last: Successful Habits of Visionary Companies* (New York: Harper Business, 1996).

4. Some Sunday morning have someone say to the congregation, "Would all of the ministers of this church who are present please stand up." How many of the laity do you think would stand? How does that make you feel? Ephesians 4:11-12 says that every Christian is a minister of the gospel of Jesus Christ and that the role of church leaders is to equip them "for the work of ministry." This simple exercise goes a long way to show where our churches are at the turn of the twenty-first century.

5. To help you with your fear while moving from in control to out of control, practice saying out loud the words that you fear the most. Why not try saying, "I'll do it because I've never done it that way before."

6. Study the many excellent examples of mission, vision, and values on our website, **www.easumbandy.com/OtherSide**, under "resources," under "frequently asked questions." Why not send me yours?

7. Visit **www.shareware.com** and explore some of the fractal software.

8. Read *Yearning to Know God's Will* by Danny E. Morris (Grand Rapids: Zondervan, 1991). How would this change the way your church makes decisions?

9. Go to **www.NewHope-hawaii.org**. This is the webpage of New Hope Christian Fellowship in Honolulu. What can you learn from their website?

10. Make a list of the ministries of your church. How many are directed outside the church and how many inside? Does your leadership deliver the gospel to the community or wait for them to come to your church?

11. I used my experiences in finding the right public restroom to describe my own difficulties traversing the wormhole. What daily experience would you use to describe your difficulty?

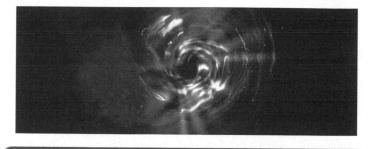

Portal 5

Spiritual Guides:
Explorers of the OtherSide

We must imitate Christ's life and his ways if we are to be truly enlightened and set free from the darkness of our own hearts. Let it be the most important thing we do, then, to reflect on the life of Jesus.

—Thomas à Kempis

For mission's sake, what if Christians were to renounce Christianity and become disciples of Jesus?

—Leonard Sweet

IMAGINE A CHURCH WHERE MORE TIME, ENERGY, AND money is spent insuring the spiritual well-being of people than on collecting dues for the upkeep of facilities. That's the kind of church that is birthed by leaders on the OtherSide.

The machine Life Metaphor of Modernity made it easy for church leaders to relate to the "church" as an institution rather than a spiritual community. It also made it easy to honor educated leaders who often ridiculed emotion and feelings. Symbols easily became the reality instead of pointing to it, machines replaced metaphor, and logic replaced passion and experience. The materialistic world was real, whereas the inner world of the soul was little more than illusion. Rationalistic materialism ruled the day.

Church leaders today appear more concerned about institutional needs than the spiritual needs of one another. Most churches today have too many members and not enough disciples; too many professionals and not enough spiritual leaders. Many of our life-saving stations have become yacht clubs. I often find more spiritual talk in a sports bar than I do in church board meetings.

However, the wormhole is changing leaders' view of reality itself. Modernity is losing its grip even in the area of the mysterious and supernatural. *As we pass through the wormhole to the OtherSide, the institutional church Life Metaphor is being replaced by a spiritual kin-dom Life Metaphor.*[1]

The English word "king" means "family leader" and has the same root as "kin." I prefer to use the term "kin" instead of "king" since it takes us to the same place without bogging us down in gender-laden issues. The mission of God's people is to grow a kin-dom of spiritual people rather than maintain an institutional church with religious people.

The following chart shows the shifts caused by changing this Life Metaphor. Keep in mind that these are not opposites or contrasts as much as blurred fragments of a paradoxical environment spiraling toward the future.

Institutional Church	Spiritual Kin-dom
Religion	Spirituality
Physical Location	Realm
Territorial Turf	May Your Tribe Increase
Bricks and Mortar	People
Budgets	Tithing
Job Descriptions	Spiritual Gifts
Programs	Processes
Denominations	Tribes
Nice Way of Life	Life or Death Issues
Operations	Missions
Internal Needs	External Yearnings

Church Work	Kin-dom Journeys
Members	Disciples
Competition	Cooperation

Institutions construct buildings, erect structures, and restructure; organisms grow people, plant deep roots, and develop relationships and networks with the environment around them. The chasm between a spiritual church and an institutional club is deep and wide. One leads to life and the other to death; one to ministry and one to meaningless rounds of meetings.

The Eleventh Commandment reads, "Thou shalt not worship thy buildings more than thy God."

The Institutional Church Life Metaphor

Institutional churches function like corporations. Pastors are CEOs. Policy manuals replace the Bible as the core document. Programs replace ministry. Pastors attend seminary and are referred to as "professionals." Denominational structures and financial needs grow faster than those of congregations. Job descriptions replace calling. Degrees are more important than proven competency. The institutional Life Metaphor is concerned with funding programs, doing church and denominational work, restructuring, balancing the budget, and repairing the buildings.[2] In such a church, leadership is based on credentials, and faith is something to be learned. This metaphor is evident in churches that place a lot of emphasis on administration, credentials, denominationalism, meetings, and defending the faith. Some examples of this metaphor can help us see the deadly effects of institutionalism.

What's on the cover of many church bulletins?—a picture of their sanctuary. Too many church members act as if their church buildings are the kin-dom and their mission in life is taking care of their facilities. God does not care about our facilities or our denominations, but God passionately cares if we are growing spiritual giants in those buildings and denominations.

It is inconceivable to most denominational officials to plant a new church without first buying land and erecting a building. The Life Metaphor is so ingrained that when churches are planted without first buying land, the members of that church can't wait until they are able to purchase land and build their own building so that they can have a real "church."

Church planting offers another example of institutionalism. It is rare for a denomination to place a new church in a fast-growing area where churches of their denomination already exist, even when those churches are dying. Such action would be viewed as competition to the existing churches.

Another example is found in the answer most pastors give me when I ask them to describe their church. Usually they begin by telling me how many members they have. Is God interested in members or servants? I can think of many ways to describe the church that would be more authentic than counting members. When asked to describe the church, why not give a description of "heart strength"? The "heart factor" could be a number of things—how many people in worship, how many in hands-on ministry, how many spiritual giants, how many people there are who pray daily for God's movement in the hearts of people around the world.[3]

The importance of place plagues God's people. People speak about the "sanctuary" as if it were holy, and children are told they should not run in "God's house." Pastors and laity alike worry too much about the survival of their building. They try to save money and keep their doors open just one more year.

Instead of building churches or worrying about members and budgets, leaders on the OtherSide focus on a much larger picture. They don't want to just make a difference; they want to be all that God created them to be and in the process change the culture in which they live.

Sanctuaries are places for birds to find safety.

The Spiritual Kin-dom Life Metaphor

Because of our wholesale endorsement of the machine Life Metaphor, spirituality has been alien to most of Western Protestantism and, surprisingly, to many Catholic leaders. Until recently, very little has been written by Protestants on the subject of spirituality. It seems more rational to speak of "religious" people and to offer courses in self-help. The historical spiritual disciplines were mostly lost during Modernity.

This loss of interest in spirituality occurred over a long period of time. The first major blow occurred when the beliefs of Aristotle became the foundation for both Protestantism and Catholic scholastics. Aristotle taught that it was impossible for human beings to have direct contact with a spiritual world because we are limited to what we can experience through our five senses. The Enlightenment went further and denied the existence of any spiritual world. In the nineteenth century, when so many advances in chemistry, physics, medicine, and other disciplines were achieved without any reference to the spiritual realm, it was a short step to concluding that science contained real truth and that the spiritual world was an illusion. Even theologians like Rudolf Bultmann believed that the gospel narratives could be understood only by demythologizing them.[4]

However, the wormhole is producing a profound interest in spirituality as opposed to organized religion. The new mantra of both churched and pre-Christian people is, "Spirituality, not religion, is my thing." People are looking for a faith with heart that connects them directly with God. Add to this a passion for the experiential and the stage is set for a fundamental change in the way people relate to institutional religion.

This passion for experiential spirituality does not stop with its effects on organized religion. It is transforming the public's views on many things such as health care,[5] education,[6] home schooling, and our search for new forms of community.[7] An examination of any good bookstore reveals that there are almost as many references to spirituality in the business section as there are in the religious section.[8] Spirituality is back in full swing except among European theologians who still dominate the United States scene.[9]

Christianity has always been about the spiritual quest of soul and spirit for the God of Jesus Christ. Leaders going through the wormhole must go back to their roots, back to the primitive—before institutions, before denominations—to the raw, miraculous, supernatural power of a runaway, uncontrollable spirituality experienced on the Day of Pentecost (Acts 2).

The Life Metaphor is spiritual, not institutional. Bricks and mortar are not our concern. Flesh and blood is at the heart of our passion. If the Life Metaphor is spiritual, shouldn't we put our church's mission statement on the cover of the bulletin, put more money into discipling people, and plant more churches? Shouldn't we see to it that more people are in mission than meetings, and more time is spent on spiritual matters than administrative issues?

Spiritual Directors

Faith was too personal during Modernity, especially in Western culture, for people to seek out the guidance or supervision of another. That is changing as we enter the wormhole. As we will see later, the emphasis on teams, community, and the end of the "heroic leader" are plowing the way for a return to an ancient tradition with a new twist. In the wormhole and on the OtherSide people will seek out the guidance of spiritual leaders.

LEADERSHIP CLUE:

Leaders function as spiritual directors or guides.

Spiritual directors are an ancient tradition that for most of Christian history has been confined mainly to the Catholic tradition. With the breakdown of Modernity, spiritual directors are gaining popularity among Protestant circles. Today, many different opportunities for spiritual direction are offered in a variety of theological settings.[10] Many denominations have a section on their web page for spiritual directors.

The leadership of spiritual directors includes four primary responses: join another on her or his journey and help them interpret her or his experience with God, help the fellow traveler identify a right path for life, embrace the supernatural, and have more questions than answers. Let us now unpack each one of these responses.

Spiritual directors join with fellow travelers on their journey in personally experiencing God's direction. They listen and guide another person in deepening the person's relationship with God, discerning God's will for her or his life, and praying for that person. They listen to the person's story and help to interpret that story in light of the biblical story. Directors suggest scripture and disciplines to the other person to deepen her or his life and make decisions that are faithful to God's call on her or his life. Spiritual directors help a person pay attention to God's personal communication with him or her in such a way that he or she can personally respond to God.

Spiritual directors are interpreters of experience, not deliverers of information. They do not delegate to others what *they* want them to do. They do not try to get them to do what the *church* needs them to do. Instead, they help others interpret what they feel *God* wants them to do with their lives and then equip them to live out their lives on behalf of the Body of Christ.

People in the wormhole seek out spiritual direction from people they trust within the Christian community. They are drawn to people who are willing to walk with them in their inner journey and help them find their way through to the OtherSide. Such guidance is given without force or prodding. All a spiritual director has to offer is an ear and a personal journey. For that, a person doesn't need any formal training, much less seminary. All that is needed is a close, personal relationship with the God of Jesus Christ and a Christian community of faith that stems from a daily experience.

Spiritual direction focuses on the relationship of the directee to God and the experiences with God that come from that relationship. It is not about ideas or solving life's problems. It is about the experiences the directees have with God's communication with them.

> Spiritual guidance is the conscious and deliberate attempt to accompany other people on their journeys to and in God. . . . [and,] in the process, to share what we have learned as we have made our own journeys.[11]

The goal of this relationship is obedience to God's call. It is based clearly on listening, discerning, and following God's word at a certain time and place in a person's journey.

Unlike institutionally-oriented pastors, spiritual directors don't feel responsible for the spiritual journeys of the people they are directing. They are not chaplains or saviors. Responsibility rests solely on the shoulders of the directee.

The further we go through the wormhole the more spiritual directors will rely on the ancient disciplines of the early church fathers.[12] There are schools that train people to be spiritual directors but at the moment most of them are in the Roman Catholic and Episcopal traditions. That will change as we spiral through the wormhole.[13] For more on spiritual directors, see the endnotes.

Spiritual directors help others identify a right path for life. Spiritual leaders engage in regular spiritual disciplines. Historically, this discipline has included prayer, fasting, retreat, journaling, personal Bible study, reflection, personal worship, centering the body in meditation, and confession. It is the practice of such disciplines that connects leaders' lives to what God is doing and wants them to hear. It is this connection that enables leaders intuitively to guide others toward better paths through the wormhole. Such leadership can't be bought or taught.

Spiritual directors, mentors, and personal guides will replace spiritual gift inventories on the OtherSide of the wormhole. Most church leaders are just now shifting from trying to find people to do the things that the church needs done to helping people discover what God wired them to do. Now the pre-Christian age comes along and deconstructs that effort. Discovering one's gifts is too final and neat. In the wormhole, we must help people interpret more than discover. In the wormhole we don't find our place in God's world as much as we find today's place within the wormhole for the moment.

Spiritual gift inventories have been a major tool for helping baby boomers find their places with the Body of Christ. Churches that have replaced nominations and committees with discernment and gift-based ministries have reached more than their share of boomers. However, the further we go into the wormhole, the less spiritual gift inventories will work.

I had a conversation with a young Christian leader during a workshop on lay ministry. We were critiquing the spiritual gifts part of the workshop. His comments are worth sharing:

> I have a problem with the statement "putting the right person in the right place, doing the right thing, at the right time." That's too neat for postmoderns. I think it is more

"an adequate person, at an appropriate place, doing whatever, for awhile."

What, if anything, will take the place of spiritual gift inventories over the next fifty years is not clear. It could be something like LifeKeys[14] or perhaps something as simple as discernment through a spiritual guide or discernment as described by Danny Morris.[15] One thing is clear, however—ministry will not be filling out forms and going to meetings. It will be bottom-up and personal, not top-down and programmatic. The focus will be on helping individuals find their God-given place in the Body and exercise their own genes instead of trying to get them to fulfill a role that the institutional church needs them to play.

Spiritual directors embrace the supernatural. The breakdown of Modernity and its dependency on the scientific and rational is opening the door for the return of interest in the mystical. Leaders reject the scientific, rationalistic, enlightened faith of the modern world and participate deeply in the spiritual, mystical, and supernatural. As a result, they don't argue the faith, nor do they try to convince people about the faith. Instead, they show them the faith. They encourage people to taste that which they cannot see, feel that which they cannot conceive of, and experience that which is beyond this world. These leaders are willing to allow the unexplained to remain just that—a mystery.

One of the clearest signs that Modernity's grip is about gone is the resurgence of belief in miracles. I like to put it this way, "If it is not impossible, God is not in it." Any deep belief in the spirit realm leads to the acceptance of the miraculous as a normal part of life. We are already seeing a renewed interest in prayer, healing, and miracles. This renewed interest in the spirit realm will continue to escalate as we travel through the wormhole.

Spiritual directors have more questions than answers. The wormhole is unlike any place we have been before. Its very presence has a way of distorting our equilibrium, causing us to lose direction. It won't be unusual for many to lose their way and still be called upon to give leadership. In such times, the best of leaders know something that many would-be leaders forget—sometimes all leaders need are the appropriate questions. In the wormhole, people seeking guidance are looking for direction more than answers.

Based on the signs of the wormhole I can think of one question that applies—WWJD?[16] Another way to think about this is to ask, "What is God already doing in this world?" and then pray to be placed nearby and run over by God's presence. The simple seeking of God's will instead of worrying about institutional needs, such as cutting the budget, fixing the boiler, or scraping enough money together to pay the pastor, might be all a leader can muster at the moment due to the severity of the ride. But that one question could help one find the appropriate path through the wormhole.

Cross-cultural Witnesses

Jesus called leaders to a kin-dom agenda. He did not call them to be pastors of churches. He called them to reach all nations. He didn't call them to chaplain a group of dependent people. Acts 6 describes how the pastor of a first-century church provided for the needs of those who needed a chaplain. Go read it.

Such a mission is far more profound than brick and mortar, enlisting members, and maintaining institutions. Instead of their mission being building churches, leaders on the OtherSide see their mission to be making disciples of all nations. Instead of focusing on how many members they have, they focus on how many people in the area around them don't know the God of Jesus Christ.

Such a mission requires leaders who feel and think differently about the mission of the "church." These leaders are called upon to be part of a spiritual realm, a holy nation, the Body of Christ, a communion of people who seek to be like Jesus.

Two of life's most immoral heresies:

"Pastor, before we go after any more new members, we need to take better care of our members."

and

"Pastor, don't you think we're big enough?"

LEADERSHIP CLUE:

Leaders think and feel like cross-cultural witnesses.

The focus of these leaders is not within the church or with the parishioners. The focus is how the church can be leaven and salt in the community around it and throughout the world. The church is no longer the place where religious things happen, but the launchpad from which cross-cultural witnesses are sent out into the world.

Cross-cultural witness leaders have three primary traits that separate them from most of the leaders during Modernity: they focus more on reaching an area than on building an institutional church, they are not tied to any one denomination or culture, and they are theologians with a clear message.

Cross-cultural witnesses focus more on reaching an area than on building an institutional church. The size of the church is never as important as the penetration of God's people into the culture in which the church is located. When they think of "church" they think of a realm instead of a place; they see a kin-dom without borders instead of a church with walls. To paraphrase John Wesley, *the world is their parish.*

In 1998, I spoke at an event sponsored by The United

Methodist Church. The event was held in a Church of God and the band and people leading worship were from the Assembly of God. While in the rest room before the workshop began, I accidently overheard a group of United Methodist clergy complaining about the event being held in a non-Methodist church. One of them was really upset about the location. When the Church of God pastor stood to welcome everyone, I wondered what he would say. To my delight he ended his welcome by saying, "We welcome all the various groups here today and our prayer for your denomination is, 'May your tribes increase, because as your tribes increase so does the kingdom.' " This pastor had a kin-dom view of "church." It did not matter to him where people went to church.

In that same year, I spoke at the New Hope Christian Church in Honolulu. They brought me in for just a day and instead of keeping me to themselves, they invited all of the pastors of Honolulu to be their guests for lunch to hear me speak. They had a kin-dom agenda that goes far beyond just building a church.

That evening I had dinner with the pastor, Wayne Cordeiro. During our conversation, I asked him, "What are you going to do when you run out of room and can't find any larger space to rent? Will you purchase property then?" (At that time the two-year-old church had four thousand in worship.) To my amazement he replied, "Well, I guess the best thing to do would be to simply close the church. By then we should have a church in every island of the Pacific and have started enough churches in Honolulu that everyone can be sent out into the world." That is the kind of response I am coming to expect from leaders who are already on the OtherSide.

We are entering an age in which kin-dom collaboration across denominational, geographical, and cultural lines will become a dominant form of ministry in healthy, effective churches. Kin-dom collaboration will center around churches and paragroups with similar visions working together to effect change in the community instead of just growing a congregation. The goal of kin-dom collaboration is to win an entire city to Jesus Christ. The goal is spiritual, not institutional.

This focus on kin-dom is also behind one of the most potentially revolutionary ministries in the United States—the many transdenominational efforts to reach large metropolitan areas. The number of parachurch groups and the multidenominational emphasis on reaching the large city is multiplying each year. Their goal is not just to convert people and to help local congregations as much as it is to spiritually and socially transform a city.[17]

Collaboration between denominations will increase as we go through the wormhole. So will the power of parachurch organizations. Present-day denominations may well be the losers on the OtherSide unless . . .

Cross-cultural witnesses are not tied to one denomination as in the past. The early stages of the wormhole are bringing an end to the short, two-hundred-year rule of the denominational era. Prior to 1958, only one in twenty-five people in the United States had left the denomination of their upbringing. Today, it is more than one in three. More and more young pastors are leaving the denomination of their upbringing and either becoming independent or choosing a denomination that offers more of an experiential faith. I see no evidence that this trend will not continue. In such an environment, leaders have to rely on their own initiatives for their education, placement, and ongoing community.

Cross-cultural witnesses are theologians with a clear message. The current drive for spirituality over religion has a dark side. Western civilization's obsession with spirituality is often divorced from any traditional, religious mooring. Its expression of faith often downplays doctrine or dogma and stresses reliance on "cosmic consciousness" or the "true self." The result is that people pick and choose a little from this tradition and a little from that tradition, creating new forms of designer faith. As people pursue experiential and mystical spirituality, they will also have a deep need for solid theology.

This is another example of the parallel between our

time and the first and second centuries. It is a time of wild-eyed experiential spirituality much like that described in Acts 2. People are testing new forms of faith. Heresy is again becoming one of the major concerns of Christians. The further we go into the wormhole, the more important doctrine will become.

We are already seeing a difference between the doctrine of the wormhole and that of Modernity. The emphasis is squarely on the redemptive power of Jesus Christ and the power of the Holy Spirit. The focus is on how the individual can live a redemptive life in which those around him or her experience the transforming power of Jesus Christ. Any form of demythologizing will prove to be useless. "Form Criticism" will be left behind. Efforts such as the "Jesus Seminar" will prove to be little more than interesting. We will return to the simple, take-it-at-face-value gospel. To many people born in Modernity such an approach will appear to be "dumbing down" the message. But to those who are drowning in a sea of gods who can't satisfy the human hunger for a divine experience, it will be a breath of fresh air.

Going Deeper

Spiritual leadership is not optional in the wormhole. Helping others grow in their faith is crucial. We are no more effective than the depth of our spirituality. The development of our spiritual lives is a primary concern.

Yet very little in the wormhole will encourage us to spend time developing our spiritual lives. Many of the products of the wormhole, such as e-mail, chat rooms, games, and MUDs are constant challenges to our spiritual development.[18] Such playgrounds are more popular than television with children and teens.

Those who enter the wormhole without habitual spiritual disciplines in place probably will not make it through to the OtherSide as effective disciples. The disorientation of the ride will destroy their equilibrium and render them useless.

I recently consulted in a great, growing church in which the pastor was working seventy to eighty hours a week. Toward the end of the seminar, I said to him, "My goal for you for the next six months is to get your workload down to twenty hours a week so you'll have more time for your own soul." I then showed him how to accomplish that goal. Three months later he called me. "I really feel guilty," he said. "Why?" I asked. "I'm not doing enough to earn my salary," he replied. I asked, "Is your home life better? Are you reading more? Do you have more time for prayer? Are you developing your spiritual life more now than before? Are you personally feeling better? Is the church growing more now than when you were doing so much? Are you spiritually more alive now?" He answered each question affirmatively. I closed the conversation with, "Then what are you worried about?"

Everything I know about leadership screams for us to go as deep in our spirituality as is possible, to *be* more and *do* less. This may prove to be one of the hardest lessons for professional, meeting-going clergy and laity schooled in Modernity to learn.

JOURNAL ENTRIES AND OTHER PAINFULLY WONDERFUL EXPERIENCES TO HELP YOU FEEL AND THINK

1. What three people have influenced your life the most? List the two most important things you've learned from them.

2. Read a classic work on spiritual discipline such as Thomas à Kempis, *The Imitation of Christ*, trans. William C. Creasy (Notre Dame, Ind.: Ave Maria Press, 1989) or Richard Foster, *Celebration of Discipline: The Path to Spiritual Growth* (San Francisco: HarperSanFrancisco, 1988). Or if you're short of time, read some selections from Richard J. Foster, *Devotional Classics* (San Francisco: HarperSan-Francisco, 1993). A short and quick read is Thomas Merton, *Spiritual Direction and Meditation* (Collegeville, Minn.: Liturgical Press, 1960).

    Read *The Spiritual Exercises* by Ignatius of Loyola. Ignatius of Loyola spent all his life working on this, which three hundred and fifty years later is still the standard for spiritual direction.

    Read about the spiritual giants of the past and present. I have found great inspiration reading about Rosa Parks, Nelson Mandela, Gandhi, and Bonhoeffer. Who are the great spiritual giants in your life? Reflect on them.

3. Try fasting once a month for a day and, as able, extend the fast another day every other month for the first year.

4. Engage a spiritual director. If you already have one, how often do you communicate?

5. Begin practicing some or all of the spiritual disciplines mentioned in this chapter.

6. Go on a two-day overnight retreat by yourself. Some of the most important things in life happen during our dreams. Many of the prophets received their visions while asleep. Don't underestimate the connection between deep contemplation, deep sleep, and God's vision. Take only your Bible and a blank legal pad. It may surprise you to know that God usually has an agenda. Do not take any "to do" stuff. There is nothing you need to "do" on this retreat other than listen to God. If it has been awhile since you have done this, you may need to add a third day or do it more than once before you are satisfied with the results.

7. Join a health club with your spouse and schedule a time for the two of you to go. What is good for the body is usually good for the soul.

8. Begin each day at home with prayer, and train folks at the church not to expect you in the office until 10:00 or later. Do not check your e-mail before praying.

9. Plan a yearly vacation and take it.

10. Develop an accountability group. This is a group of people that you trust to objectively give you feedback on your ministry. Meet with them regularly. Ask them to hold you accountable to what you are called to do. Perhaps give them a two-by-four with your name written on it. If you're like me, sometimes you're so headstrong that you remind yourself, and them, of the proverbial mule.

11. Ask a group in the church to pray for you. Studies are showing that people in hospitals who are prayed for

do better even when they do not know people are praying for them.

12. Some high-charging people need more than one day off a week to recharge. If you are not a one-day-off-a-week person, take regular time away from ministry. Every four weeks or so, my wife and I would "get lost" for four or five days. This worked for us better than a day off each week. Talk with the leaders of your church about customizing your time off to suit your personality.

13. Listen to your favorite music. The younger a person is today, the more likely music will be a major form of renewal of the soul. My spirit soars when I hear music like "My Prayer," "Majesty," "God of Grace and God of Glory," and believe it or not, "I'll Fly Away." What music fills your soul and turns you on to the wonder around you?

14. Find a mentor. Mentors help people avoid making some of the mistakes they've made. One of the problems of being a pastor of a church is that often one is stuck in an area where one may be the only spiritual giant around. Who do you have around you that makes you run on all cylinders?

15. Did you read Acts 6? Does it have anything to say about your leadership style?

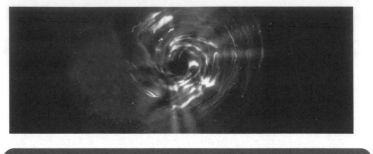

Portal 6

The Lone Ranger Was a Team Player

Command and
Control Committees .... Permission-
Giving Teams

A quiet revolution is taking place. ... Management is heading toward a new state of mind—a new perception of its own role and that of organization. It is slowly moving from seeking power to empowering others, from controlling people to enabling them to be creative.
—Perry Pascarella

IMAGINE A CONGREGATION WITH SELF-ORGANIZING teams and no nominating committees, where nothing is ever voted on and decisions are based on prayer and discernment, where everything stems from and is measured by the DNA, and so much is happening that no one person or group is in control. Such is the church that emerges from leadership on the OtherSide.

Once the organic spiritual Life Metaphor takes the place of the institutional mind-set, reality is viewed more as a web of connections than a world of boxes and lines. The top-down practice of command and control gives way to a permission-giving atmosphere in which teams function autonomously.

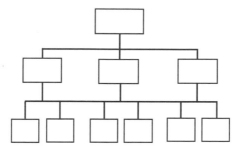

Organisms are always connected in some way to the environment around them. Faith is always connected to another. First God, then others. Faith is never simply for ourselves. The rugged individual concept is flawed. So is the idea of individuals acting in isolation from one another. Entrepreneurial pastors are only as effective as the teams they assemble.

The day of the heroic leader is under severe attack and is coming to an end as we spiral to the OtherSide.[1] Charismatic, lone wolf leadership is too one-dimensional to be effective in a world of speed, blur, and flux. Because of the nature of the wormhole, teams will be far more effective.

I don't mean to imply that heroic leaders are not needed in the wormhole and won't exist on the OtherSide. It's just that they won't be the most effective type of leadership in most cases. A number of major corporations are already experimenting with three CEOs.

In *Growing Spiritual Redwoods,* Tom Bandy and I referred to leadership as an event in which the effectiveness of spiritual midwives was in direct proportion to how well they helped others birth the gifts within them.[2] On the OtherSide there is much less room for individual, charismatic leadership.

One of the primary reasons the last fifty years of Protestantism has produced so few spiritual giants is Modern Christendom's practice of putting new members to work on committees before they have been discipled. Instead of encouraging them to engage in "soul work" they attempt to involve them in "church work." They try to get them active on a committee instead of "abiding in Christ." They want them involved in the machinery of the church instead of discovering the heart of God. They assume because they have joined the institution that they feel and think God. They worry more about how they spend their time than what's in their hearts and minds.

In the early stages of the wormhole, we are witnessing a shift from a command and control Life Metaphor to a permission-giving, team-based Life Metaphor. The shift does not seem to be understood by many church officials raised in Christendom. Most church officials think that all they have to do is call a committee a "team" and they have made the transition.

In 1991, Roberta Hestenes wrote a book in which she gave advice on how to turn committees into teams.[3] Most people by then knew that committees were draining the life out of congregations and denominations, but no one seemed willing to dump them. So, Hestenes decided that she would try her hand at offering a solution.

However, in 1998, Hestenes did a tape for the Pastor's Update from Fuller Theological Seminary in which she says that she now realizes it is foolish to think of turning a committee into a team.[4] More and more people are finding that out.

In 1986, the church in which I was serving Christ threw out most of their standing committees, (at the time we had over 350 people on committees, as was required by our denomination) and went to what we called "Ministry Teams." I wrote about the transition in *How to Reach Baby Boomers.*[5] The year we went to this system our ministries quadrupled in number and quality. I have seen these same results in hundreds of churches in the past decade.

Comparisons	
Command and Control Committees	**Permission-Giving Teams**
Committees Are Elected	Individuals Are Called

Committees Are Nominated	Leaders Invite the Team
Standing Groups	End When Task Is Done
May or May Not Have a Mission	Have a Clear Mission
Are Not Autonomous	Are Autonomous
Have to Clear All Actions	Are Free to Act Within Boundaries
Are Not Accountable for Results	Are Accountable for Results

The Command and Control Committee Life Metaphor

During Modernity, two kinds of people made most congregations function—those who made decisions and those who carried out the decisions. A centralized group of elected officials dreamed up programs they thought would help the church grow and then looked for some poor schmo who could not say no. Often, people would take on the responsibility simply because *their* church asked them to and they would feel guilty if they refused. The same people who made the decisions also controlled the election process of those who were to serve on the committees that carried out the decisions.

Committees are so ingrained in the fabric of established church life that most leaders can't conceive of a church without committees. One lady said to me, "If the church didn't have committees, how would we involve people in the church?" Involving people in committee work was the Life Metaphor.

> *Committees seldom develop spiritual people, much less spiritual giants.*

Because of the command and control Life Metaphor, most churches have become little more than places where members live out a perpetual spiritual adolescence. Church members seldom become disciples in a controlling environment. Leaders have to give up control for others to take responsibility for their actions. Until that is done, no one reaches their potential. They just vegetate their spiritual lives away.

The primary thing that is holding churches back today from shifting from command and control committees to permission-giving teams is the desire of some leaders for power and control.[6] However, that is swiftly changing. More and more churches are discovering that most people born after 1970 prefer not to be the "out in front" leader but prefer to work in teams with other leaders. Their Life Metaphors are different.

The Permission-Giving, Team-Based Life Metaphor

The digital age is breaking down the hierarchical, command and control model of Modernity. It is easier now to share enough information throughout an organization for everyone to have all the information needed in their area of expertise or spiritual gift to act on behalf of the total organization. Since the wormhole challenges every part of the system to constantly transform, it is not enough anymore for a leader just to lead—everyone in the system must lead in his or her area. People at every level of the organization must be moblized to assist in the revolution of how we think, feel, and do ministry. To do that, they need information.

Those who make the decisions also carry out the decisions. Instead of a centralized group who decides what happens, permission-giving churches spread decision making throughout the church, freeing everyone to live out their spiritual gifts without asking for permission, as long as what they feel called to do enhances the agreed upon mission, vision, and values (core values or purpose) of the church and they can find two or three others who want to share in the ministry.

Permission-giving churches replace centralization with autonomous, permission-giving teams.[7] Giving permission to informed teams to function autonomously is the fastest way to respond to a world set on blur. Companies are already showing that by employing cross-functional teams they are able to cut production time in half. Permission-giving, team-based churches are experiencing the same multiplying phenomenon.

Permission-Giving Leaders

It was not until 1995 that I wrote about the permission-giving church.[8] The reason it took so long for me to write about it is that before I started consulting with other churches I did not realize how controlling most church leaders were. I thought that all I had to do was show them how to grow the church and they could implement it. Was I surprised! After more than one hundred consultations, it was clear to me that one of the biggest obstacles to the growth of people and the church was *control.* What made it even more surprising was the fact that every church with which I worked was filled with good, salt-of-the-earth people. But almost every church had at least one controller who intimidated the others and controlled the work of the Spirit. (I've never seen a church with more than a handful of mean-spirited controllers.) Authentic leaders control only to the extent that they keep the ministry and discipleship on target with the mission of the church. Permission-giving leaders are willing to take on mean-spirited people and transform them or ask them to leave. You can't live with cancer in the body.

LEADERSHIP CLUE:
Leaders are permission-giving.

Two key traits characterize a permission-giving leader who can function well in team-based ministries: this leader sees in others what God sees in them, helps them discover it and then gets out of the way, and insures that each person is discipled before being placed into leadership.

Permission-giving leaders see in others what God sees in them, help them discover it, and then get out of the way. One of my memorable experiences with permission giving came in the early 1970s in the church where I served Christ for twenty-four years. At this time, large numbers of refugees were fleeing Vietnam. In order to come to the United States they had to have a sponsor. A new member of our church approached me one day with the idea of sponsoring a Vietnamese family. It sounded good to me because one of our values was social justice and what he wanted to do enhanced our mission, so I told him he could do it, if he could find enough other people to help him. Over the next twelve years we sponsored over one hundred refugees from around the world, and the ministry was never voted on. Did we make some mistakes? Sure. Would we do it all over again? You bet. Would we have ministered to so many refugees if we had voted on every issue? I doubt it.

The story of Christ Church in Fort Lauderdale, Florida, is a story about permission-giving, team-based ministry. A layperson wanted to begin a ministry to the homeless. He approached the pastor, Dick Wills, about the possibility and Dick told him the ministry fit the church's third core value of relieving suffering, so he could do it, if he could find two or three others who wanted to do it with him. The layperson went off, cast his vision, and eighteen months later he and more than one hundred and fifty other laypeople had established the second largest shelter for the homeless in Broward county.[9] The church never voted on the team or the project. Most churches would have killed the project either by voting it down or by submitting the idea to an existing committee that would have debated its merit and most likely dropped the idea as being too risky.

What makes leaders like Dick Wills so effective in the wormhole is that they try to discern whether or not the "call" from God is actually from God. For him, the issue has to be a very specific kingdom-oriented issue and not just something that does not violate the core values of the church. As such, the new ministry is normally too big for any one person to accomplish without a team, and even then it appears to be possible only if God is in it.

The difference between permission-giving team players and controllers is amazing. The following is a composite of these differences that was collected from comments shared by several people on one of our online forums.

Permission Givers	Controllers
Trust People	Don't Trust People
Risk Takers	Play It Safe
Look for Vision and Excellence	Look for a Résumé
"Why Not?!"	"Why Do You Want to Do That?!"
Future Is More Important Than Past	Past More Important Than Future
Failure Is a Learning Experience	Failure Means It Was Wrong/Bad
Intentional Learners	Believe They Know Enough
Both/And	Either/Or
People More Important Than System	System More Important Than People
Learn from All Sources	Use Our/Denominational Resources
Live without Clear Maps of the Future	Want to Follow Proven Trails
Comfortable with Uncertainty	Want Guarantees Before Beginning
Relationships	Rules and Regulations
Grace	Law
Now	Later
Learn from Mistakes	Don't Make Mistakes
Learn from Doing	More Information First
Evaluate	Dominate
Collaborate	Dictate
Set Free	Keep Hands On
Confident	Fearful

Open to Holy Spirit	Locked in on Own Agenda
Don't Know All That Is Happening	Need to Know All the Details
Open to Surprise	Want All Predictable
Energize Others	De-energize Others
Mentor Others	Order Others
Welcome	Screen
Listen	Deaf
Group Purpose Is Guide	Self-Agenda Is Guide
Macromanage	Micromanage
Celebrate Others' Success	Compete With Others
Care About Growth of Others	Care About Getting Their Way
Team Builder	Team Boss
Gentle	Harsh
Worship God	Act Like God
Humble	Presumptuous
"How did it go?"	"Did you get approval first?"

One of the primary benefits of permission giving is that spiritual wallflowers start to blossom. Churches are filled with spiritual wallflowers. Few people blossom because of attending a committee. When you see people blossom after sitting in the pews for years, when you see them exercise their gifts, when you see the joy in their eyes, you know the benefit of permission giving. You also realize it's biblical.

The Internet is one of the best examples of how permission-giving organizations are going to function. It is totally out of control. Where is it? Who controls it? Can it be censored? These are questions that no one knows the answers to.

The Internet has been doubling every year since 1988 with no signs of slowing down. Such progression could not happen in a controlled environment. Instead, the growth of the phenomenon has been spontaneous, haphazard, uncontrollable, out of control and self-managed—reminiscent of pre-Christian times.

The Internet teaches us several things about permission-giving organizations of the future. (1) The worst thing to do with an organization in a fast-moving world is to try to control what is happening. (2) The role of the middle manager is being replaced by disconnected individuals who know how to use the system. (3) The healthy organization is flexible and does not have a central point of authority (keep in mind that this organization has its mission, vision, and values firmly in place). (4) The system functions as long as those who use it are trustworthy. Viruses can destroy the whole fabric of this emerging society, just like nuclear bombs could destroy the world. (5) The larger the organization the less it depends on its macro aspects and the more it depends on the micro aspects. Individuals and teams are more important than massive organizational and hierarchical charts boasting lines and boxes. (6) In such an organization no one person is in charge since it is too complex a task. Trinitarian-like teams of complementary leaders will guide this organization into the future. The role of the "senior pastor" will be less and less evident. For more information on "permission giving" see the endnote.[10]

Permission-giving leaders make sure people are disciped before placing them in leadership. Leaders on the OtherSide deploy no one before their time. They know that the further we go into the wormhole, the less likely people will have a personal relationship with Jesus Christ. The more important it will be to place people in an atmosphere in which they can grow before they serve. Assimilation by committee is coming to an end.

Training and equipping the leaders of the church is one of the primary responsibilities of all key leaders, paid or unpaid. The key role of the lead pastor is the selection and equipping of the paid staff. The key role of the paid staff is the equipping of the leaders they gather. The key role of the unpaid leaders is the equipping of those on their teams. Helping people grow into spiritual giants is one of the primary roles of leadership in the wormhole and on the OtherSide.

Team-Based Leadership

The Lone Ranger had Tonto and Silver. Batman had Robin and the Batmobile. The Green Hornet had Kato and the . . . I can't remember the name of the car, can you? (I can just hear the Modernist say, "I can't believe he would leave a blank in a book.") Team leadership is the best vehicle in the wormhole.

I first wrote about team ministry in *How to Reach Baby Boomers,* in 1991.[11] At the time, I focused mainly on what I called "ministry teams." These were self-governing, autonomous teams that came and went based on the interests of people or the demands of the moment. The longer these teams functioned, the more apparent it was to me that teams of competent people, not necessarily heroic leaders, could accomplish more without much supervision than could any one of the most competent people on my staff. It became clear that the best leadership at all levels of an organization—top, core, or bottom—is a form of team-based leadership. The farther we travel into the wormhole, the more convinced of this I become.

LEADERSHIP CLUE:

Leaders are team-based.

Team-based leadership knows that: ministry occurs best in teams; building community is essential; integrity, competency, and consistency are the basic characteristics of good team players; triad leadership is often better than one heroic leader; leaders choose their successors; many of these leaders will be women.

Leaders know that most ministry throughout the church occurs best in teams. Unlike committees, teams are never nominated and elected by majority vote. Teams are best put together by the leader of the team. Say a person wants to start a shelter for the homeless. In a permission-giving system this person is free to begin this ministry if it fits into the mission, vision, and values of the church. Permission can be granted by any leader of the church. This person begins looking for a team by casting his/her vision about working with the homeless. The leader assembles a team of people who really want to help the homeless and are willing to give their time, energy, and money to make the shelter a reality. The team plans and carries out the strategy without interference from above. If the team runs into problems, it solves them without interference from an outside committee or person. The team is free to carry out the ministry any way it deems appropriate, even if it has never been done that way before. If the homeless ministry is successful, the church may make it a core ministry and put it in the church budget. If the team messes up and does not do what it was commissioned to do, the team leader is held accountable.

Teams never meet to decide what they are supposed to do, never have to convince a member of the team if the team should do the ministry, never have to waste time debating the merits of the projects. Teams can direct all of the energy to making the ministry successful.

Permission-giving team-based churches look at people not as new blood or new money, but first as spiritual souls in need of nourishment and then as candidates for ministry. Personal and spiritual growth, rather than involvement or activity, is their goal.

The team Life Metaphor believes that laity are empowered only when they are equipped to serve others. Laity are encouraged to follow their gifts, not the organizational needs of the institution. Autonomous teams carry out the mission of the church without interference from the top. Accountability is more important than control. Control is having to ask permission before doing something. Accountability is doing something and then being held accountable for it based on the mission, vision, and values of the church.[12]

However, my task is not to describe the how-tos of team-based ministry but to show their important connection to leadership. Those wanting to know more about team-based ministry can refer to the endnotes for more information.[13]

Leaders exemplify and build community. Traveling

through the wormhole is proving to be a lonely experience for several reasons. First, the ride will separate the courageous from those who live in fear of change. Second, those pastors on the fringe of denominational life will be singled out as "troublemakers" or "mavericks" to be avoided because they do not do it the way it has always been done. Third, the world is already far too fragmented. Almost one out of two people today under the age of thirty-five has grown up in a divorced home, without a stable, healthy family environment. The only sense of community most of them have experienced has been with the peers they "hang with." In such a world, the rediscovery of community is basic to the life of the people of God.

Christianity is community. From the beginning, Christianity has focused on the importance of community. The primary aspect of the Trinity is that God exists in relationship, not in isolation. Therefore, it is only natural for Christians to function best in community with one another.

Community is impossible without trust. If trust exists, we have little need for so many checks and balances in our church policy. When we are in community (trust), permission-giving systems are normal. When teams are added to the equation, community life explodes with new life in the presence of new ministries that bubble up from the congregation instead of coming down from the top.

Trust=Community=Permission-giving+
Team-Based Ministries=Ministry Explosion

The Web is becoming one of the great communities of the wormhole. Many church people frown on these communities and say that they will never replace in-person communities. They simply cannot imagine a virtual community.

Our organization has several online communities. One of them has taken on the character of an authentic community. Not long ago the wife of one of the regular contributors miscarried. Prayers poured out for the couple. People who lived nearby gathered at the their home to support them. When the wife became pregnant some months later, people rejoiced.

Several times a year a post will appear stating that a forum participant is attending a conference in some city and designating a place for anyone on the forum who is attending the event to gather. Authentic online communities find ways to have face-to-face fellowship. It's the nature of communities to do so. To sign up for one of these listservs see the endnote.[14]

Cyberchurches are already forming. In time they will catch on and become major communities in the future. See the endnotes for two websites.[15]

Spiritual leaders know that people are made to live in community with people who follow the God of Jesus Christ. Community is not a luxury; it is essential. The church of Jesus Christ must exhibit how to live in community with Christ and one another. The need for community and family is one of the most important things young adults are looking for today.

You know you have found Christian community when serving one another is more important than activity, involvement, and volunteers; accountability and discipline are modeled instead of control and policies; people bear one another's burdens; there is freedom to fail; trust abounds; and loving relationships are the goal.

Leaders know that integrity, competency, and consistency are crucial. One of the keys for successful team-based ministries is trust. Without trust, teams cannot survive, much less thrive. Trust depends on several key characteristics on the part of the leaders involved.

Competency: Those who function in a team have to be able to count on the other members of the team to do what they say they will do.

Consistency: They have to be able to count on the other team members to be there for them.

Integrity: They have to be able to take team members at their word.

Triad leadership at the core will be the most effective form of leadership in the wormhole. The time has come for congregations to experiment with multiple lead pastors with the same DNA but different genes. The speed at which things occur in the wormhole suggests the importance of a leadership team at the core of an organization. The challenges faced in the wormhole are too complex and varied to be addressed by one person. A good team of leaders working in concert with one another, bringing different perspectives and gifts to the table, is better than the singular heroic leader of Modernity.

The Trinity provides a powerful image of triad leadership. The image of God in the Scripture is three-dimensional—creator, redeemer, and sustainer, or Father, Son, and Holy Spirit, whatever works best for you. If you compare this to what is needed today, the *creator* is the doer or activist who gets things accomplished, the *redeemer* is the transforming nature of the change agent, and the *sustainer* is the shepherd who cares for the souls. It is rare for one person to have all these gifts.

George Cladis has provided us with a wonderful insight into the relationship of the Trinity to team-based ministry. In his book *Leading the Team-Based Church,* Cladis says:

> The divine community of the Trinity provides a helpful image for human community that reflects the love and intimacy of the Godhead. Hierarchical distinctions in the human community give way to a sense of the body of Christ, with each part equal and important (1 Cor. 12-14). The individual persons of the church are distinct parts yet are bound together in a common sharing and loving relationship. . . . If we do not move toward an image, a goal, of spiritually meaningful and effective team ministry, our failure will surely result in relational breakdown, the result of human sin.[16]

The Trinity points to the importance of relationships and the interconnectedness of everything. Relationships are a key issue in the wormhole. In the final analysis, all that will matter is our ability to show the world a community of people who live by different rules. It really is true—high tech requires high touch.

Leaders are involved in choosing their successors. Where choosing one's successor is most acute is with the change in lead pastors with long tenure. Two types of leadership tenures are emerging as we pass through the wormhole. Among the older travelers who are successfully making their way through the wormhole the tenure of the lead pastor is proving to be twenty or more years. Among the younger travelers who are making their way successfully through the wormhole, the tenure will probably be shorter—say, ten years. In either case, the replacement of the leader of leaders will be more crucial than ever before.

Once churches consciously begin to function around their DNA (mission, vision, and values) they do not need another strand of DNA emerging with the advent of a lead pastor who has a different DNA. They may need a pastor with different gifts, but not different DNA. Enough confusion exists in the wormhole without conflicting DNA.

How can leaders respond to the need to participate in securing the lead pastor's successor? Churches with call systems will find this easy to accomplish. Just become clear about the mission, vision, and values of the church. Then, before the long-term pastor retires, begin looking for the successor. Allow the outgoing pastor to participate in the choice. Then require the outgoing pastor to step out of the picture as much as the incoming pastor wishes. Denominations like The United Methodist Church are the least prepared to cope with the issue of succession.

However, it is not just the succession of the lead pastor that is important. Every leader needs the freedom to select and groom her or his successor. A leader always needs to be grooming a successor. Remember fractalling? This is the only way to insure against multiple strands of

DNA. Remember, just because the new leader has the same DNA does not mean that person is a clone of the predecessor. The person's genes insure that even though the DNA is continued, it will be done according to the personality of the new leader.

Many of the new leaders will be women. During Modernity, the prevailing leadership model was a white, male, individual, entrepreneurial, win/lose type of thinker. Feeling was not important. It was a very concrete world with very tangible results. Community was not considered as important as bank accounts. This worldview required females, who played a supporting role. It also required certain kinds of "inferior" males to play their subordinate supporting role. In the wormhole, much of that is changing. Feelings are back. Community is essential. Intangibles are more important than concrete facts. Intuition is often more valuable than knowledge. *And* women have had enough domination.

Modernity: "Now since our preacher can't be everywhere, we are going to start this new ministry."

Wormhole: "Sorry our ministry teams couldn't be everywhere, you'll have to settle for the preacher this time!"

Moving Toward Permission-Giving, Team-Based Ministry

I am often asked how churches begin to move toward a permission-giving, team-based ministry. Although it takes time, pastors can begin the process by simply giving people permission to experiment with ministry without getting any other form of approval. If a controller challenges them on it later, they can always ask for forgiveness.

Usually, pastors spend a year or two laying a foundation for permission giving by casting a vision and reacquainting people with the Scriptures. Soon they start giving a little permission here and there, saying, "Just try it and see how it works. See how many other people are interested in it, then go for it. When you get a little success under your belt, we'll go to the board and let them see it." Many of these new ministries will do very well, which helps lower the fear level among the leaders.

However, sooner or later churches have to agree to move into this model if it is going to reach its full potential. Permission giving can't reach its potential in a traditional, voting-based congregation. It takes major transformation and the dropping of most existing structure. It also takes trust and mutual respect among the leadership.

Two behavioral changes must happen for permission-giving systems to flourish. First, pastors have to give up control of ministry and begin equipping others for ministry. Second, laypeople have to give up control of the administration and begin to do most, if not all, of the pastoral ministry.

It is impossible to move into a permission-giving system without causing some anarchy in the congregation. However, most people in a congregation don't care how the church functions as long as their needs are met. Most of the core leadership will see the wisdom in the move to a permission-giving team structure. Only a small percent of the leadership will see it as anarchy or confusion because "we've never done it that way before" and it may lead to their loss of control.

However, it's really not anarchy. It's freedom! When you give people freedom in the Spirit, they blossom and so does the church. Diversity replaces conformity. Your leaders don't all look, smell, and think alike, but they're all about the same mission. The have the same DNA but a different cellular structure.

The following steps have proved helpful to churches in moving from an institutional, committee-based model to an organic, permission-giving, team-based ministry.

(1) Whenever possible, give people permission to try new things, and if it backfires ask for forgiveness for not knowing better. It is easier to get forgiveness than permission.

(2) Whenever possible, let out-of-date programs or committees die instead of working hard to prop them up.

(3) Whenever possible, reduce structure.

(4) Reduce required staff attendance at noncrucial meetings.

(5) When possible, give new ideas to newly appointed teams instead of standing committees.

(6) Pastor, start setting your own agenda instead of letting individuals in the church set your agenda.

(7) Begin immediately to find ways to replace all of the controllers with positive and objective people who share the large hopes and dreams of the healthy people in the congregation.

How Does One Know?

You may be asking, "How do I know whether or not the situation in which I am serving/leading is one which might become a permission-giving, team-based organism? The answer is that transformational leaders never know for sure. However, it is helpful to have some ways to measure the success of transitional efforts.

Commit to paper the following three measurements: (1) the objective measurements you are going to use to help you decide where to begin the change process and determine if you are making progress; (2) the length of time you are willing to invest in this place; (3) the amount of yourself you are willing to invest. Keep in mind that the personality and gifts of the leader have some bearing on the length of time it takes to transition a church and the amount of success the leader will have. Give yourself three to five years to know if the transition is taking place and monitor your own feelings to see if you are personally going to be able to handle the stress. A case study will help you get started.

"Anywhere Church" has five serious controllers without whose approval nothing happens. As a result, a considerable amount of tension and conflict are present, causing most of the new people to not stay around very long. Over the past few decades, the church has experienced a slow, steady decline. Since Pastor Sally knows that it is impossible to do anything about transitioning a church without first dealing with the conflict and the controllers, she writes down the following objective measurements: *Reduce the amount of conflict. Develop a healthy community life. Replace the controllers with healthy spiritual leaders.* Next, Pastor Sally decides she will give herself a year for these measurements to take shape.

At the end of the year, the community life is stronger than the conflict and the controllers have been replaced with healthy leaders. Pastor Sally is now ready to move to the next level of transition.

Pastor Sally takes an inventory of her emotional and physical strength. She concludes that because of her young age, she is willing to risk most of her emotional strength and much of her physical strength for the sake of the transition because the rewards on the OtherSide of the inevitable pain of transition are worth the personal investment. She also does an inventory of the willingness of the new leaders to transition into a permission-giving, team-based ministry. Based on the inventory, she proceeds to work in those areas that are open to change and to change those areas in which people still have concerns.[17]

Two years later Pastor Sally has a clear picture of the success of her ministry. New ministries have been instituted, the worship attendance is growing, new leaders are surfacing, and the church is becoming a permission-giving, team-based congregation.

When people are allowed to work in teams around their spiritual gifts on projects that are important to them, they are more likely to grow into servants rather than mere volunteers. That is the subject of the next chapter.

Journal Entries and Other Painfully Wonderful Experiences to Help You Feel and Think

1. Think of the last committee meeting that changed your life for the good. On the other hand, think of the last committee meeting in which you considered never going to church again. Think of the last time you served on a project that actually helped people. Which one of the above was the most fullfilling?

2. What risks do you see in the permission-giving, team-based form of ministry?

3. What risks do you see if you continue the command and control form of ministry?

4. Visit a couple of cyberchurches to experience online community.
   www.firstcyberchurch.orgn/evangelism
   www.websyte.com/PositiveChurch

5. Sit down with your eight- to twelve-year-old and enjoy the following community-building experience. Go to **www.mamamedia.com** and find Mamamedia. It offers eight to twelve-year-olds an opportunity to learn how to use the web and lets them create a personalized Internet experience.

6. Have your leaders take the Permission Giving Readiness Test in *Sacred Cows Make Gourmet Burgers.* Where are your weaknesses and where are your strengths?

7. What was the name of the Green Hornet's automobile? If you can't remember or are too young to know, go to

www.moose.uvm.ed/~glambert/green.html. You can find it there.

8. Make a list of the committees your church wouldn't miss if they didn't exist. Discuss the list with the more mature leaders of your church.

9. Make a list of the committees that are causing harm to your church. How? Why?

10. What committees can the leaders agree to drop at this point?

11. What committees can you agree on that are absolutely necessary to your church? Why? Could their activities be done by a team instead?

Portal 7

Whose Church Is It, Anyway?

Elected Entitled	Called Discipled
Members . . . . Servants

An adult is trying to hook up a computer. His four-year-old strolls into the room and asks, "Want some help?"

Very truly, I tell you, the one who believes in me will also do the works that I do and, in fact, will do greater works than these, because I am going to the Father.
                                                                —John 14:12

IMAGINE A CHURCH WHERE NONMEMBERS ARE ENTITLED to everything a church has to offer and the members are servants who have given up all entitlements. That's the kind of church birthed by organic, spiritual, permission-giving, team-based leaders on the OtherSide.

Effective churches on the OtherSide raise the standards for membership so high that only servant leaders join. In a way, membership becomes the gateway to leadership. The OtherSide requires high-commitment churches. We're already seeing the emergence of these churches. In almost every case, the number of people in worship outnumbers the number of members.

The institutional Life Metaphor makes it easy for church members to feel entitled to a vast array of amenities, and the primary way to serve is to sit on a committee that basically services the well-being of the members—a rather arrogant stance for people called to "take up the cross" (Mark 10:21 KJV).

Israel fell victim to the same arrogance. The people of Israel believed that as long as they kept the harvest and full moon festivals Yahweh was their God and they were entitled to Yahweh's protection. However, God chose Israel for a special mission—to be a light to the nations. She was special because she was chosen for a divine mission. She was not chosen because she was special. Over time Israel began to think of herself as being chosen because she was special. The difference between being special because you are chosen and being chosen because you are special is enormous. One is servanthood, the other entitlement.[1]

In an entitled system, membership, not servanthood, is the primary goal. It is easy to distinguish a pastor locked in the throes of Modernity by simply asking, "What size is your church?" How the pastor answers gives a clue as to the pastor's relationship to the wormhole.

On this side of the wormhole:
"Pastor, what size is your church?" The response: "We have over one thousand people on our rolls. Our budget is $500,000. We have ten staff people. Our building covers seven acres." (Church is measured as "members, buildings, dollars.")

In the wormhole:
"Pastor, I'm interested to know how many different people you have in worship during one whole week." The response: "Well, I guess if you count our satellite coffee worship services, our house worship in different neighborhood houses, and worship in the sanctuary, it could be about one thousand people. That doesn't include our radio/TV ministry, of which we don't have firm figures. And it doesn't include people in the

armed services, college, and so forth who receive our worship materials via Internet." (Church is measured by the number of people worshiping God as a community).

On the OtherSide:
"Pastor, I'm interested to know how many pre-Christian people your faith community is able to reach each week with the gospel message." Response: "Well, that's a good question. We have several systems in place to train every disciple to be a disciple who grows other disciples who grow other disciples." (Church is measured by the quantity and quality of the way the disciples are sowing the word and bringing in the harvest.)

In the last gasps of Modernity, membership became equated with discipleship. Once a member, spiritual development became optional. In the past few decades most members have opted out of any form of personal spiritual development. They mostly sit and soak.

However, a new day of discipleship is dawning. The elected, entitled member Life Metaphor is being replaced with the discipled servant Life Metaphor. In the wormhole, leaders have to make personal sacrifices. It is no longer good enough to sign up and then never show up.

The Entitled Life Metaphor

The entitled Life Metaphor is the most deadly sin of the twentieth-century church. Entitlement takes many forms: the person in the hospital who is not satisfied with a visit from a "mere" member of the church, but insists that the "head" pastor visit; the person who gets upset when someone sits in *his* pew or parks in *her* space; the person who gets angry on Easter because so many people show up that it is difficult to get around in *his* church. The entitled church allows people to join and participate on their own terms. Members have rights. Representation is everything. Personal opinion reigns. Activity and involvement are king. Pastors lobby for better pensions, parsonage or housing allowances, a forty hour work week, and are more concerned with keeping their parishioners happy so they can keep their jobs and feed their families than they are with whether they are living out their call.

One of the most heretical forms of entitlement occurs in the way church leaders relate to their pastors. The entitled Life Metaphor believes pastors are "hired guns" brought in by the church to do the ministry of the church on behalf of those who pay their salaries. "Pastor fetch" is a primary role of the clergy. Whatever the members need them to do pastors are supposed to do. After all, this is "their" church. With such an entitled mind-set, pastors are expected to do all the spiritual work of the church, such as baptisms, communion, weddings, funerals, praying, visiting the sick, counseling, going to meetings, and supporting the denomination. In a Bible-based, servant-oriented church these ministries can be done by anyone who is part of the Body of Christ.[2] However, the institutional church finds it difficult to understand this.

Membership in the entitled Life Metaphor works in two directions. When a person joins a church, the present members of the church feel entitled to get something from that person. Often this "something" is help in supporting the budget and performing some ministry that no one in the church wants to do. On the other hand, the people joining feel entitled to some privileges. Often these "privileges" involve getting first crack at putting their child in the weekday child care, being able to have their daughter married in the church, free use of the building, and access to the "head" pastor whenever they want it.

The biggest sin of my ministry was allowing my peers to convince me for a season that the democratic, representative form of government was the way to run a church. It is so nonbiblical, I can't believe I fell victim to such folly. But I did, and I assume many of you have also.[3] It is time to end the folly.

The Servant Life Metaphor

Churches moving to the OtherSide are dropping the nonprofit term "volunteer" in favor of the biblical word "servant." This switch is not merely a change of names. The entire ethos of the church on the OtherSide is changing. Servants are held accountable to the mission, vision, and values of the church. Leadership is a privilege offered only to the most committed, and most of the ministry is done by the congregation.

Servanthood, not membership, is the goal, and everyone is encouraged to serve based on their gifts. Leaders have to meet certain requirements before being called to lead. It is not unusual in these churches for leaders to be required to tithe, lead a ministry, be in a small group, and be present in the monthly gathering of the leaders with the pastor.[4] Servants are called, not elected. Servants are raised up by God, not a congregational vote. They naturally respond to human needs by choice, instead of waiting to be asked.[5]

Churches who have reached the OtherSide no longer hear the words "I'm just a layperson," and pastors no longer make the mistake of saying they "entered *the* ministry."

I mentioned the trend from volunteer to servant in my first book, *The Church Growth Handbook*. Only then, instead of using the term "servant," I used the terms "paid staff" and "unpaid staff." Although the terms "paid staff" and "unpaid staff" referred to the same shift as volunteer to servant, I regret that I didn't use the biblical term "servant." It would have gone a long way to lessening the traditional commitment to the questionable concept of clergy and laity. About all the clergy/laity distinction accomplishes is a caste system that devalues most of the people in the Body of Christ. It's time we abolished most of our clergy/laity talk and once again talked about the servant people of God and the Body of Christ.

Churches who have made it to the OtherSide are learning that a seminary education does not guarantee a servant pastor. For some reason, a seminary education seems to make it more difficult for a pastor to have a profound sense of servanthood. Seminary-trained clergy have a professional air about them. In some traditions, they even go to "professional meetings."

It always shocks long-standing church members when they learn that Bill Hybels, pastor of the largest church in the United States, has only one semester of seminary. Just the other day, a young man told me, "Life is too short, and delivering the Word too important, to waste it sitting in a classroom." "Instead," he said, "I'm going to do what Jesus did, and get on-the-job training."

Most churches on the OtherSide are finding that the fewer seminary-trained clergy on the staff, the healthier the church. For this reason I am telling growing churches not to have an associate pastor until they reach five or six hundred in worship. In a church where membership leads to leadership, people don't expect the pastor to be the primary caregiver, so less clergy are involved.

When Mao Tse-Tung took over, there were two million Christians in China. His regime killed the missionaries, arrested the pastors, shut down the churches, and persecuted the Christians. When he died, there were fifty million known Christians in China.

Because of the growing professionalism of clergy and the increasing affluence in developed countries, wormhole leaders are being forced to look for mentors in the third world, where being a servant often requires sacrifice and obedience to a radical gospel.[6]

Leaders are learning from third world leaders that: God needs servants, not professionals.

God wants obedience more than success.

God honors radical devotion to disciple making.

Wealth is not in what one possesses but by whom one is possessed.

Using one's gifts on behalf of the Body is more important than getting a degree.

One hour a week in worship does not a Christian make.

Prayer is essential to the journey.

Small groups are vital to the discipling process.

The world does not revolve around Western Christianity.

The authentic Church is always countercultural.

LEADERSHIP CLUE:

Leaders serve Jesus Christ in the midst of a congregation instead of serving a congregation.

This distinction is crucial. It's what keeps leaders from merely taking care of people and allows them to grow people. Ineffective pastors make a fatal mistake when they think they're supposed to serve the congregation. When that is their goal, they become like Aaron, whose claim to fame is that he helped the rebellious Israelites build a golden calf. Many pastors today are building golden calves instead of pointing people to Jesus Christ.

In order for leaders to be able to serve Christ instead of the congregation, leaders must: represent Christ by modeling the faith, be real people who aren't concerned with being nice, and have the soul of both poet and prophet.

Leaders represent Christ by modeling the faith for others to see. Jesus taught us that modeling is the most natural and basic teaching technique we have. Children, without even trying, naturally learn the complicated task of language from role models. The same is true at church. People learn what we model far better than what we say. Do not be surprised if over the next few decades intentional modeling among the great leaders of the church replaces much of the role now played by institutions such as seminaries and Bible Colleges.

These leaders find fulfillment not in what they accomplish but in what they help others accomplish. They don't look for followers; instead, they see in others the potential that God sees in them and help them birth their own leadership. Their goal is to equip people to tackle their own problems and create their own future, not follow the leader's vision.[7]

> Imagine the differences in behavior between leaders who operate with the idea that "leadership means influencing the organization to follow the leader's vision" and those who operate with the idea that "leadership means influencing the organization to face its problems and to live into its opportunities."[8]

Studies are showing that the more leaders encourage those around them the more leaders emerge. The Center for Creative Leadership did a study of leadership in which they found that what distinguished the top performing manager from the bottom was the amount of affection given to them by their supervisor. The closer their supervisor was to them the better they performed.[9]

According to Ephesians 4:11-12, pastors are set aside to "equip the saints for the work of ministry." Spiritual leaders don't serve a church; they serve in order to help others grow in Christ. For many, this requires a major retooling. Church leaders must go from "doers" to "equippers," from "teachers" to "facilitators," and from "bosses and employees" to "team players." These distinctions alone separate the spiritual giants from the rest of the flock.

It's time we called the decline of our churches what it is— a failure to grow strong Christians. Pastors, we've allowed people to vegetate, to become little more than pew potatoes. We've made domesticated house pets out of them and have refused to let them out of the sandbox. We've made their lives shallow and unproductive by leading them to believe that the role of the clergy is word and sacrament and that their role is to make decisions. We've done for them things that we should have equipped them to do. We've stolen from them their spiritual birthright, and for that our churches are little more than hospices where people wait to die and hope to God that the money doesn't run out before they do. Is that the legacy we want to leave?

Leaders are real people who aren't concerned with being nice. Leaders are both saints and sinners. They express their emotions, including their anger. They make mistakes and above all, they don't seek perfection or think of themselves as holy or even good. If you think about it, most of the primary characters in the Bible were stinkers. Consider Jesus' statement, "Why do you call me good? No one is good but God alone" (Mark 10:17).

I'm convinced that most church people think that one of the tenets of Christianity is being nice. Too many church people think pastors should be nice people and churches are supposed to be nice places where people live harmoniously together. As a result, most church leaders never really say what they feel or think, which leads to a loss of community and a handful of dysfunctional controllers who keep the majority of people intimidated. Niceness leads to the withholding of information, manipulation of people and events, and gossip. I've discovered that the most dangerous gatekeepers often appear to be nice.[10]

Why is not being nice so important that it is included in the list of leadership clues for the wormhole? Because most dying churches have a handful of people who need to be kicked in the butt. That's why.

I've seen a disturbing pattern throughout all of my consulting ministry: most established churches are held hostage by one or two bullies. I keep hearing pastors say, "If I tried that, I'd lose my job!" Some individual or small group of individuals are usually extremely opposed to the church making any radical change, even if it means the change would give the church a chance to thrive once again.

Courageous pastors often ask, "What do I do when one person intimidates the church so much that the church is not willing to try something new?" My response is always, "Either convert them, neutralize them, or kick them out." To which someone usually cries, "That's not very Christian!" What they mean is, "That's not very nice."

My response describes much of the wisdom of both the Old Testament and Jesus. Maturing Christians love so deeply that they will do anything, even not be nice, "for the sake of the gospel." Jesus was so compassionate toward others that he could not remain quiet when he saw people holding other people in bondage. Jesus called his best friend "Satan" when he got in the way of the mission. He drove the money changers out of the temple. He went out of his way to upset the religious bullies of his time.[11] Being nice is often nothing more than a lack of compassion for people. Church leaders are robbing people of their spiritual birthright when they allow dysfunctional people to bully the church.

One of the basic lessons I'm learning as a consultant is that before renewal can begin, some person or group usually has to leave the church. Almost every time a dying church attempts to thrive once again, someone tries to bully the leadership out of the attempt. Almost every time, if a turnaround is to take place, these people are lost along the way because they are no longer allowed to get their way. When they can't get their way, they leave. Not even Jesus got through the journey with all of the disciples. Why should we expect to? For information on how to deal with dysfunctional bullies, see Matthew 18:17.

From Linda Bergquist

What follows is really more of a hope than a prediction. It will probably take some transitional people to get us in the ballpark. The people who will take us through the wormhole will probably be:

1. Missionary: Besides breaking through the usual barriers of ethnicity, culture, and economics, they will also transcend and bridge worldview gaps between modern and postmodern believers. The East is becoming so missionary across cultures that it positions the West to address Western worldview shift.

2. Honest and vulnerable: open to cross-generational mentoring, ready to lay all their tools and methods, and even their reputations, down, only picking up what God calls them to take on the next phase of the journey.

3. They will do everything they can do to address their generation so that the generations following can better address the future.

So what about when we have an indigenous postmodern leadership on the OtherSide?

1. Still missionary: A lengthy time of transition is ahead. Also, the world is changing so fast that we cannot afford to school people as methodologists, but as missiologists.

---

2. Biblically more holistic: learning to acknowledge biblical themes that modern Christianity has all but ignored.

3. Relational and spiritual authority rather than positional authority structures. Also, natural emergent leadership from those structures.

4. Diverse and nontraditional roles--not just pastors and staff people, but leaders who help us see beauty through the arts, lead us to be disciplined about our bodies, lead us to appreciate the creativity and wonder of God through nature, and so forth.

5. More bivocational and team leaders sharing leadership responsibilities, especially in organic expressions of church life. Higher value on community.

6. Values driven rather than purpose driven or goal driven.

7. Not so much anti-institutional as noninstitutional.

8. Evangelistic in a more holistic manner. Expressing Christ--not just telling of him.

9. Leaders will come with baggage from unhealthy families and be in need of mentoring--wounded healers ministering out of their weaknesses.

10. Communication and faith will sometimes be symbolic: piercing and tattooing as suffering servant identification with Christ, poverty vows to take on the burden of the poor, celibacy vows to protest the degrading role of sex in the culture. High commitment acts.

11. More diversity in the culture of what it means to be Christian. Many more Christian subcultures, some even tribal in nature.

12. Less difference theologically between charismatics and other evangelicals. Charismatics needing to be fully versatile in scripture, others more open to a supernatural God—both needed for evangelism of postmoderns. Biblical knowledge and experience merging in revelation. Strategy and spirit meeting in intentionality.

Linda Bergquist is a postmodern pilgrim of boomer vintage, living in San Francisco, working as a church starter strategist in the Bay area.

Leaders are both poet and prophet. The center of the wormhole requires a paradoxical leader. On the one hand leaders must be as sensitive as a poet and on the other hand as brash as a prophet. Wormhole leaders must be able to articulate and express the soul of the congregation and at the same time apply the Word of God directly to the lives of the people. They must be able to weep with those in need and combat those who would bully others into submission.

Poets and prophets have one thing in common that is essential in the journey to the OtherSide—they offer people hope. Hope is a precious blessing at the center of the wormhole—the promise of a new day on the OtherSide.

Journal Entries and Other Painfully Wonderful Experiences to Help You Feel and Think

1. Does your church require your pastor to play "pastor fetch"? If so, do you think this is the biblical way for a pastor to spend her or his time? Can you think of ways to change this picture?

2. Go to **www.kindness.com/matrix/matrix.htm** and discuss with some group in your church which of the suggestions for servant evangelism you find the most helpful. Then do the same with a few unchurched friends.

3. When was the last time your life was blessed the most—in church or doing something that helped someone else?

4. Pastor, take gifted laypeople with you to the hospital every time you go. Let them observe you and then debrief them on what they saw and how they felt about the visit. When you feel they are comfortable with the idea, let a layperson lead the visit and afterward ask how the person felt about it, what questions the person has, and whether this is something that brings fulfillment to him or her. If so, when you think the person is ready, ask him or her to make some hospital visits in your place and then debrief the person on how it went. Do this with other gifted people in your church. Let those who excel and find the visits really fulfilling become the primary caregivers to anyone in the church who will let them. When you are ready for the congregation to take over all of the hospital ministry, take them with you on the first visit and introduce them to the patients as their primary carepersons until the patients fully recover.

5. Write down the names of the handful of people who control your church by intimidating everyone. Why are they allowed to do it? What might happen to them if they were held accountable for their destructive behavior?

6. Make a list of the people in your church you consider to be servants. Are you satisfied with the length of the list? Would you like to have more? What can you think of that your church might do to encourage more servants?

7. What are your church's requirements for membership? Are they high enough? Is your church open to making membership the gateway to leadership?

8. What would happen in your church if you talked about replacing the nominating committee with either prayer or spiritual gift inventories? What has been your experience with paid staff members? Which are more effective—ordained or nonordained people?

Portal 8

Almost to the OtherSide

This Side . . . . The OtherSide

When the student is ready, the teacher will appear.
—Ancient Asian Proverb

We do have an advantage over any other time in history. When other profound change took place, those living through it tended to be unaware of the historical significance, and were aware mostly of the transition pains and difficulties. We are fortunate enough not only to be able to watch major change take place within a single lifetime, but also to possess enough knowledge to have a good picture of what is going on. Our pain in it can be exhilarating and fun. Given the choice, why not perceive it that way?
—Willis Harman

I can do all things through him who strengthens me.
—Philippians 4:13

IMAGINE A WORLD THAT RESEMBLES LITTLE IF ANYTHING of the world 2000. That is the world on the OtherSide.

So, what do the following have in common?

Television
Nuclear energy
Space travel
Computers
World Wide Web/Internet
Automobile
Air travel
Quantum physics
Air-conditioning
Refrigerators
Indoor plumbing
Inoculations against many diseases
Women's rights
Civil rights
Wireless communication

They all occurred during my mother's lifetime.

My mother was born in 1910. She has seen the above changes either discovered or reach their zenith during her lifetime, but she has witnessed only two things that have the potential to change history as much as the discovery of fire or the wheel.

Which two of the above do you think have the potential to change everyone and everything in the world? **Which one do you think is in the process of doing that right now? Choose the right one and you might finish the ride.** Take a moment and see if you can find the basic clue to the future.

Record your decision_____

What one thing can be said about people born on the OtherSide that can't be said about people born before 1980? People born after 1980 were born into a digital world. This one distinction will separate them from every other person born before them—just as the printing press did, only much faster. They are growing up digital, interactive, holographic, and virtual.[1]

The Internet could have a more profound effect on the course of human history than all of the other discoveries or inventions combined.[2] The only thing that will not be fundamentally changed by the Internet will be our relationship to Jesus Christ.

LEADERSHIP CLUE:

It's not what leaders know that is important; it's what leaders know is not important.

The information society, spawned by computers and the Internet, is glutting the world with more data and information than most people can handle. Data are little more than indiscriminate, disjointed, and often pointless scraps of facts and figures. The proliferation of new "junk" websites every second and the constant flow of mindless chatter on listservs is just the beginning of this problem.[3] Information, on the other hand, is timely, connected, and useful. Leaders need to be able to shift through the junk without being affected by it and share with other leaders the information pertinent to them, giving sound leadership.

The issue becomes more complicated when the Internet becomes embedded into everything that exists. What do I mean by the embedded Internet?

The 1918 Sears catalog devoted several pages to announcing the sale of a five-pound motor for $8.75. This electric motor was first promoted as a stand-alone, like the Internet today. It could be used to run a number of products, such as turning an old icebox into a refrigerator. The electric motor became a cultural icon. Sounds silly, doesn't it? Today, it is embedded into the products when we purchase them. The same thing is happening today with the Internet. In a very short time nanotechnology will produce such a tiny and inexpensive chip that the Internet will be embedded in everything and everyone.[4] It is already embedded in automobiles, refrigerators, dogs, and cats. In time, every human will have the opportunity to become embedded. Parents will have their children embedded so that can't get lost or kidnapped. Children will have their aging parents embedded so that they can never wander off.

LEADERSHIP CLUE:

Leaders need a clear sense of what it means to be human.

Spiraling to the OtherSide, we cross what Bruce Mazlish calls the "fourth discontinuity."[5] Kevin Kelly describes the fourth discontinuity in this way:

> We are now crossing the fourth discontinuity. No longer do we have to choose between the living or the mechanical because that distinction is no longer meaningful. Indeed, the most meaningful discoveries in this coming century are bound to those that celebrate, explore, and exploit the unified quality of technology and life.[6]

The possibilities will be staggering when the advances in the biomedical field reach the point of embeddedness. Machines will continue to become more human and humans will continue to be more engineered, thus more machine-like. It will become more difficult to define "human." Many scientists already believe that life, reduced to its simplest form, is little more than a computational function. Can't you just hear someone in the future asking, "What does your computer want?"

In 1958, the first cyborg (part human, part machine) was created in the United States when a human being received the first heart pacemaker. Since then, our level of "borgness" has been growing with no sign of abating. In time, perhaps even the human brain will be replaced with a synthetic apparatus.

Electronic communication will compound the problem. From MUDs, where people develop multiple personalities, to e-mail, to highly developed and personalized evangelistic avatars in chat rooms, more and more people's primary form of communication and interaction with others is the electronic media. This leads to two questions: are electronic representations our true selves; and what does a faith like Christianity, one that is grounded in the idea of incarnation, tell us about what it means to be human in this increasingly disembodied or disincarnate time? Leaders will be called upon to answer these and other questions not yet asked.

LEADERSHIP CLUE:

Leaders need to be able to help others distinguish reality from fiction.

If your head isn't spinning yet, don't worry, the ride isn't over. Remember those commercials that included deceased stars, such as Humphrey Bogart and Lucille Ball, in the same scene with current-day stars? Remember how real they looked? Add to this the development of commercially viable virtual reality and holographic imagery, and determining what is real and what is virtual will become impossible for the human eye.

Now, consider the implications when the emerging world of virtual reality goes embedded. Instead of "going" to church, will many just "enter" church through their computers? Technology now has the ability to create worlds that can actually fool our senses. We got a Hollywood look into such a world in the movie *The Matrix.* The role of leaders in such a world will be one of truth telling: helping people see beyond the fictions they've created for themselves to see the world the way God sees it.

In such a world the issue of soul and what is real will become of paramount importance. Leaders will be called to address the difference between machine and biological beings, as well as what is real. Whereas the baby boomer (born 1946–1964) wants to know, "What do I do after I've had it all and it's not enough?" people on the OtherSide want to know, "Which faith is real?" or "Which clone has the soul?"

Church leaders have to get people to face the world as it really is, and that means facing the reality of a dying church. Such reality will cause pain. Such pain always causes resistance at first, but the role of leadership is to help people face reality and to mobilize them to move past the pain and transform their community of faith.

Of course, one wild card could be played that will change all of this. We could experience a nuclear war. That is the second item from the list that could change the course of history. If that occurs, all of the above is out the window, at least for the next ten thousand years or so. If that occurs, leadership will be a moot point, so I'm not going to pursue this path, although the probability of a nuclear war scares the hell out of me (no other way to describe my feelings).

We're almost done now. Only one thing remains—we need to begin changing our Life Metaphors. The next chapter is devoted to that challenge.

Journal Entries and Other Painfully Wonderful Experiences to Help You Feel and Think

1. What part of the "embedded" world don't you like and why? Which parts do you like and why?

2. What implications of "embeddedness" do you feel will influence your ministry the most?

3. How do you feel now about the OtherSide?

4. Go back to the early chapters of this book and review some of your early feelings about the wormhole. Have they changed? Do you feel more comfortable or uncomfortable?

5. Review your understanding of the word "church" from when you began reading this book. Has it changed? If so, how? If not, why not?

6. Watch the movie *The Matrix.* What are some of the information databases you would like to upload into your brain instantaneously? What part might spirituality play in discerning the difference between the knowledge of a subject and the wisdom of how to use it?

7. Can you name a movie or a television show that gave you a spiritual experience? Is the world providing better spiritual experiences than the church? Are there secular movies that help you connect with the "sacred"?

8. For a fun experience go to **www.X-files.com**.

9. For another fun experience go to **www.whatisthematrix. com** or **www.home.telia.no/torlokken/thematrix**.

Portal 9

Remain Seated With Your Seat Belt Buckled: The Ride's Not Over

If I accept you as you are, I will make you worse; however, if I treat you as though you are what you are capable of becoming, I help you become that.

—Goethe

He led me all around them; there were many lying in the valley, and they were very dry. He said to me, "Mortal, can these bones live?" I answered, "O Lord GOD, you know." Then he said to me, "Prophesy to these bones, and say to them: O dry bones, hear the word of the LORD. Thus says the Lord GOD to these bones: I will cause breath to enter you, and you shall live. I will lay sinews on you, and I will cause flesh to come upon you, and cover you with skin, and put breath in you, and you shall live; and you shall know that I am the LORD."

—Ezekiel 37:2-6

A T THE BEGINNING OF OUR RIDE TOGETHER, I promised to mess with your mind to help change your image of the "church." I hope I have kept my promise.

If you've stayed with me on the ride, you've begun to see that the way the word "church" is used by most people today is close to heresy. So much so, that our use of the word "church" has become a primary killing field for leadership. I think this heresy is now the primary reason why 85 percent of established churches are on a plateau or are declining. Our inadequate understanding of "church" has decapitated our understanding of leadership.

So, what does the word "church" describe based on the new Life Metaphors? *It describes people who are called by God to take part in a mission from God led by people who are passionate about the mission.* God first sought a relationship with Israel for a specific purpose—to be a blessing to the rest of the world and to restore the broken relationships between God and the creation. Israel would be God's chosen people if, and only if, they chose to carry out God's mission.

God called Abraham and told him that he would be blessed and through his efforts all the nations of the earth would be blessed. God's people were chosen and blessed so they could bless others. This covenant was continued in Isaac, Jacob, and then years later in Moses.

Unfortunately, Israel turned inward and chose not to be a blessing to others. Over time, she felt she was God's special, chosen nation. She began to feel entitled. So God went looking and Jesus appeared.

Jesus called Israel to task over her loss of mission. Parable after parable spoke of Israel's defection from the mission. Jesus' accusations against the established religion of his day increased until the day he said, "The kingdom of God shall be taken from you, and given to a nation bringing forth the fruits thereof" (Matt. 21:43 KJV).

Could this be what is happening today in many established congregations? Could it be that God is abandoning them in favor of those more willing to assume the mission along with the blessing? God's call is a call to mission. Salvation is not something primarily for you and me. Salvation is for us *and* for those who will be blessed by us. The church is composed of people on a mission from God.

The meaning of "church" and "leader" should now be

clear. *Churches are places where God's mission is carried out, and leaders are those who equip the church to carry out that mission.* Therefore, where there is mission, there is the church. Where there is no mission, there is no church.

Those churches that exist simply to underwrite the budget or keep a pastor so that they can survive long enough to care for the remaining remnant of members do not meet the criteria. At best, they're hospices; at worst, they're clubs; but in no way can they be considered churches. Some are museums that exist to perpetuate the memories that have piled up in the brick and mortar. It is time we owned up to our sin. It is time denominational officials quit propping up these hospices, clubs, and museums.

It is also time that leaders led. If you're in one of these institutions, get the hell out of there. Now! As fast as you can. Run for your life before you lose it for nothing. Find a place where people are open to God's mission and lose your life in that mission. Find a place or plant a church where people will allow you to focus outward on the world. Too much is at stake for you to continue to do the routine maintenance of archaic institutions. *When the horse is dead, dismount.* My friends, the horse is dead. Dismount!

Imagine and Create Your Future

The real challenge facing Christian leaders is to change the fundamental assumptions on which they create images of reality (i.e., what we think and feel determines how we see the world around us and how we respond to it). Change the way we feel and think and we can change the way we act. In other words, becoming a leader means that most of us will have to change our Life Metaphors.

The ability to change your Life Metaphors depends on

your passion level—how much passion you have for the mission.

Remember the very first clue we discovered at the beginning of our journey together. *Leaders are obedient to a call greater than their own lives.* Your passion for a God-given mission has to be more powerful than the congregation's pull on you to merely take care of them.

LEADERSHIP CLUE:

Leaders are willing to change their Life Metaphors.

Here's the good news—anyone can change their Life Metaphors if they want to badly enough. For those ready to attempt to change their Life Metaphors, the following suggestions are one way to begin.

The first step is to recognize that you have Life Metaphors and that they may be the reason you aren't as effective as you'd like to be. Spend time in prayer and Bible study. Prayer and Bible study are great starting places for people in search of new Life Metaphors. Too many of our Life Metaphors are shaped more by cultural mores than by biblical realities. What many think is the "gospel" is little more than cultural Christianity that has little to do with the gospel. So spend some time reading the Gospels. Go back to the point at which you first began your spiritual journey. Remember how you felt and why you started the journey. What were the early events that shaped your life?

Second, name the Life Metaphors that affect you and decide if you *want* to do something about them. This would be a good time for you to refer back to the unwritten assumptions, rules, policies, and prejudices that are holding you back from doing what is necessary to live up to your calling. If you did not write them down earlier, do so now and record them in your journal. Make a list of the changes you feel you need to make.

Third, if you've decided you want to change your Life Metaphors, then right now challenge all of them

and begin to act just the opposite of them. Throw them out for now and see what materializes as you dream of a preferred future without them. New and challenging ideas usually emerge over time based on how thoroughly you have actually set those Life Metaphors aside. But remember, doing this may disturb your equilibrium as well as those around you. Doing so should cause you to think and feel differently and that may raise some eyebrows. You might even lose some friends or your job.

Fourth, be willing to be a lifetime learner, which means constantly retooling as the mission demands it. You must allow your experiences to be gateways into new images of reality. Remember, ultimate authority today is experience and the ability to interpret it for yourself as well as to help others interpret their experiences. Leadership is not about what you know. It is about who you can help interpret God's movement.

The next step is to decide if you're willing to pay the price to change your Life Metaphors. Changing your Life Metaphors will result in a change in your basic beliefs. You may not be the same person. The stronger your belief system, the harder and more painful it is to change the Life Metaphors. Most people find this process so painful that they drop the issue, so be sure you want to do this. Those who are successful in pushing through the Life Metaphors usually do so because the pain of not carrying out their calling is more painful than changing their Life Metaphors.

The final step is to begin imagining a new reality. Ask yourself, "What if I did live up to my calling? What would I have to change?"

One way to imagine a new reality is to change the questions you are asking. Let me suggest four questions that can profoundly change your style of leadership.

Instead of "What am I going to do today?" ask, "Who will I mentor today?"
Instead of "What is my job?" ask, "Who will I discover?"
Instead of "How much can I do?" ask, "How many others can I equip?"

Instead of "Who can I disciple today?" ask, "Who can I equip to go and disciple others?"

Reshaping your Life Metaphors around these four questions can't help preparing you to be open to the kind of leadership demanded on the OtherSide.

From Mark Driscoll

Organic missional leaders in our postmodern, post-Christian, poststructural world are a tribe defined not by the answers they hold but by the questions which hold them. The following is a glimpse into the content of their dialogue.

What does it mean for the church to be local, global, and historical?

How was Modernity not only a failure but a sin?

Why must a Trinitarian theology reject the modern view of the autonomous self?

What are the windfalls and pitfalls of postmodernism?

Why is the beauty of God essential to life?

Why is biblical narrative theology overtaking systematic theology?

What does a Christian community look like in terms of architecture, multiple family dwellings, and so forth?

How can the church transition from a senior pastor to a ministry team?

How is worship a form of evangelism?

What is the difference between being missional and doing evangelism?

How was cessationistic theology an outgrowth of atheistic naturalism?

What is the difference between mysticism and being charismatic?

How will networks replace denominations?
Why is chasing pop culture trends both foolish and fruitless?
How can ministries transition from being program driven to being community driven?
What have Western Protestants lost in abandoning their Catholic, Orthodox, and Hebrew roots?
How can the church transition from giving data that are informing to giving experience that is transforming?
Why should church health precede church growth?
Why must the church depart from a business identity of providing goods and services to religious consumers?
What were the specific errors of Descartes?
How can the church avoid both syncretism and sectarianism in the postmodern world?
What is the difference between reason and rationalism?
How are the religious right and left missing their opportunity to be missional?

Mark Driscoll is pastor of Mars Hill Church in Seattle, Washington.[1]

The Bible is full of people who have experienced dramatic changes in their Life Metaphors. As you study them, you will notice that in each case there's an intervention. God intervenes with a vision of something different and better than what existed.

The key to changing your Life Metaphors is to put yourself in the path of God's vision for your life and quit listening to what others tell you to do. Don't follow the rules just because they're the rules. Be willing to dream and imagine a world where your life makes a drastic difference. Then ask, "What do I have to change to live up to that vision God has for me?"

If you are contemplating messing with your Life

Metaphors, I strongly suggest that you invite a mentor to join you in your journey. Your efforts are usually more productive. That's one reason we have free forums on our website. We want to help you find spiritual partners in your journey.[2]

One Last Hope

My greatest hope is that once on the OtherSide, Christian leaders don't make the same mistake that was made in the fourth century A.D. and revert back to an institutionally-driven, machine-oriented, propositional faith. That would be the greatest tragedy and travesty I can imagine.

So, join me in this prayer:

God, put me in the path of what you are doing in this world. Show me where you are working. Run over me with your presence and guide my path to the OtherSide.

Journal Entries and Other Painfully Wonderful Experiences to Make You Feel and Think on the OtherSide of the Wormhole

1. What were the early events in your life that shaped your Life Metaphors? Write them down.

2. Describe in detail your earliest recollections of God in your life. Did the experience leave you feeling as if God had something for you to do with your life?

3. What would your life be like if you were totally fulfilling your understanding of God's will for your life?

4. Read the stories of God's intervention in the lives of Abraham (Genesis 12–18), Jacob (Genesis 27–35), Moses (Exodus 1–4), Lydia (Acts 16), and Paul (Acts 9). What are the similarities? What do you see in their lives that might spark God's intervention in your life?

5. Begin to record the images that have been exploding during our ride together. Do you see ways that they will change your life?

6. For a fun and educating time see **www.bigquestions. com**, but be prepared for the pages to take time opening.

7. Who do you need to go to and confess your sins?

8. Has the horse died? If so, are you ready to dismount?

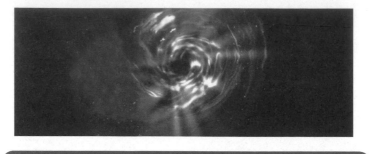

Welcome to the OtherSide

CONGRATULATIONS! YOU'VE FINISHED THE RIDE AND apparently are still in one piece. I trust the time you invested was well spent. It's now time to wrap this up and put it to bed so you can go out and equip disciples who equip other disciples. But before you do, let's take a good look at what life might be like on the OtherSide.

What We Can Guess About the World on the OtherSide

It is impossible to predict what life will be like on the OtherSide of the wormhole. However, every good navigator has to have some reference points from which to get her or his bearings. So consider the following thoughts as MegaClues about the future. I don't expect any of them to pinpoint reality, but I do expect people alive in 2015 to be able to see their reflection in the world around them.

MegaClues for Society

1. The religious and secular worlds will continue to blur in every way except one—religious beliefs

and values, which will be crystal clear due to the resurgence of the prominence of the Scriptures.

The pre-Christian world will continue to blur all boundaries. The world will be seen by individuals as either all secular or all sacred. Matter and Soul will be merged into a holistic approach to life. On the other hand, the beliefs of effective leaders and churches will continue to become more focused and uncompromising. Already, the churches with the clearest and most focused beliefs and values are reaching the most pre-Christian people.

2. The clash between the old and the new will shape most of the first two decades of the twenty-first century in almost every area of life.

This will be especially true in well-established congregations. Civility will continue to wane, and angry people will take out their frustrations on their neighbors as we have been seeing in the random shootings at school and on the highways. As the Gen X and Y generations reach into the power systems ruled primarily by boomers, this clash will be one of the worst in history. The winner will be the Gen X and Y generations because they are the best at the new technology.

3. The Internet will continue to grow until it is the primary form of communication, information, commerce, and networking throughout the world.

First, the embedded Net will be the number-one way communication takes place and information is gathered in the twenty-first century. It will replace the fax, the postal service, and Ma Bell as we know them.

In this global/tribal, multicultural world, the Internet is becoming the vehicle for both worldwide and grassroots communication. It promises to offer us the best chance to respect and nurture some of the most obscure languages and cultures of the world. The cross-cultural exchange will be enormous. It will allow people in the most remote areas of the world to communicate with people across the planet in different languages because of web browsers that automatically translate languages.

Second, vast amounts of information will be free and uncensored. The size and location of a church will have nothing to do with the amount of information at its disposal. The smallest church will have the same information at its fingertips as the largest church. In time, the Net will provide any size of church with all the music it needs to conduct any kind of worship service it wishes. In a very short time, both the financial restrictions and the learning curve needed to use the Internet will be as cheap and easy as opening a phone book.

Third, it will be the major form of commerce in the twenty-first century. The church of the future will advertise primarily on the Net. I now download more magazines than I buy; it's cheaper and I don't have to have all those magazines cluttering my home or seat on a plane. The embedded Net will be the Sears catalog of yesterday and the mall of today. Our organization already offers all our materials on the Net, within twenty-four hours, at 40 percent off the printed price. People no longer have to wait for "snail mail" to deliver their purchases, and churches overseas can receive the materials the same day.[1]

Fourth, and most important, the Net is a vehicle for networking, mentoring, and interaction between congregations. A whole new form of ecumenism is developing where the stress is not on doctrine or denominational organization but on learning about and sharing ideas on effective ministries. New forms of alliances, partnerships, networks, and worship are emerging because of digital technology. House churches are getting their curriculum from the Internet.[2] More and more of the great teaching churches are sharing their ministries on the Net, allowing churches in the process of transition to see a wide variety of options from across the world.[3] In time, the Net will provide more training than the traditional seminary and perhaps make it obsolete.

Our organization provides several networking forums for church leaders. With the click of the mouse, you can subscribe and begin communicating with a wide variety of church leaders from all over the world with similar interests and missions. You will find this option on our website, **www.easumbandy.com**.[4]

4. Religion and science will become more like kissing cousins than alienated enemies.

The introduction of quantum physics has changed the Life Metaphors of many scientists. Very few believe anymore that science holds all the answers to the riddles of life and the universe. Scientists and theologians are now seeing the interconnectedness of everything in creation. The more organic the world becomes, the more logical a place religion will have in the role of science.[5] The door is now open for exploratory conversations between the two disciplines.

5. Biogenetics will become the primary theological battleground replacing today's flash points of gay rights, abortion, and gender.

"Homo technicus" is already replacing "Homo sapiens." It seems as if every month a new gene is discovered that has a direct bearing on how people behave. Everything from congeniality to criminal impulses to IQ to sexual preference is being attributed to our genes. *Nature* is slowly becoming more important than *nurture.* The neuroscientific view of life is moving to the forefront of the academic world, and if we are not careful, society will begin worshiping at the feet of biogenetics, making us slaves to our genes. This is not a good scenario for the future.

In 1999, British Telecommunications began working on a chip that can be implanted in the brain to enhance human memory. The project is called "Soul Catcher."[6] In late October of 1998, doctors at Emory University implanted a device into the brain of a paralyzed and mute stroke victim allowing him to move a cursor across a computer screen and point at icons conveying simple messages. Is this a hint as to how people in the future will send e-mail, turn on the lights, open doors, and have conversation?[7] Talk about extrasensory perception.

Personal computers are becoming more human. A new kind of digital imaging chip, or "silicon eye," is already able to process vast numbers and images as fast as PC chips now process words and numbers. Companies are beginning to use fingerprints for passwords, and by the end of this century some computers will feel our touch and respond. HNC Software develops artificial "neural net" applications that allow computers to "think."[8] Their goal is to develop neural nets that can read, interpret, and search text, recognize sounds, and scan and interpret images. Researchers at Irvine Sensors Corporation have discovered how to pack silicon chips so tightly that they can connect enough of them to mimic the connection density of the human brain. Imagine what this could mean if combined with the "neural net"?

Add to the above a project under way at Massachusetts Institute of Technology on finding ways to allow computers to express emotions. "Affective computing" software will allow a computer to adapt to its user's mood as well as pacify its frustrated user.[9] About all that is left is for researchers to figure out how the human brain works and then it will be all over—machines will have the capacity to become more human and humans will have the capacity to become more machine-like. As we enter the OtherSide, we can expect to see the evolution of both machine and organism into a cybernetic culture.

The future implications of genetics on Christianity should be a cause for concern, for several reasons. First, experience teaches us that many church leaders will respond to the successes of genetic engineering in one of two ways. Either we will ignore it or we will approach it as our enemy and ignite another religious fight against science. We know all too painfully how neither response prepares us for the future.

Second, it will hasten the day of the "posthuman" or "cyborg" mentioned earlier. Third, it gives people a wonderful cop-out for their sins. Can't you just hear, "My genes made me do it"? This is my greatest fear about the present work in genetics. We humans don't need any more excuses to avoid taking responsibility for our lives.

I first wrote about the importance of genetics on Christianity in *Dancing with Dinosaurs* when I referenced the Human Genome Project.[10] Over the next few years, the entire human gene pool will be mapped out. We already know that there are about 5,000 genes that could be fundamentally affected by our present drugs. Futurists are already speculating as to when parents-to-be will be able to select the specific genes they prefer in their baby-to-be. What is human and what is real will be two of the ethical issues of life on the OtherSide.

6. If it doesn't entertain, stimulate, and touch all of the senses, it won't educate or be worshipful.

Edutainment is now one of the mainstays of people born after 1965. The word "edutainment" is already the name of a popular catalog that targets educators.[11] *Sesame Street* began the trend in 1969 when it launched a truly revolutionary method of combining education and entertainment.[12] The trend in children's education continues to become more entertaining with programs such as *Barney* and *Blue's Clues.* Church leaders will have to get over their bias against entertainment if they want to communicate the gospel. Of course, the opposite is true— entertainment without the gospel is meaningless— however, no more meaningless than many of the worship services I've seen lately.

7. Three-dimensional holographic organizational charts will replace the flat organization of the 1990s.

The 1990s were the decade of the flat organization, restructuring, downsizing, decentralizing, and reengineering. The OtherSide will give depth to what is now flat. A 3-D, holographic chart will allow an organization to see the multiple connections that run throughout that organization, as well as the relationships it must nurture inside and outside the organization.[13] Holographic imagery builds the whole of the organization into every part, encouraging fractalling. It fosters the networking of emotion and intelligence. It rules out fragmentation, compartmentalization, bureaucracy, and as much hierarchical structure as possible. In such an organization no more is defined than is absolutely necessary.

8. Society will continue to become more hostile to local congregations and more open to spirituality.

One of the assumptions I made in my book *Dancing with Dinosaurs* is that the hostility between organized religion and society would continue to escalate. I still hold to that view. Church leaders in most parts of the country are learning how difficult it is becoming to get a permit and zoning to build, add on, or purchase more adjacent property. Secular enterprises never have as much trouble.

9. The primary search is for wholeness, community, dignity, identity, and empowerment.

Pre-Christians are not joiners. They aren't going to belong to our churches simply to belong. Modernists might think that pre-Christians would find identity and community in institutions—but not so. Now people find community and identity in the stories shared by their fellow travelers. Community and identity are formed by one's connection to a shared metanarrative within the Christian community.

10. People will play books instead of reading them.

The history of putting our thoughts on paper, beginning with hieroglyphics on the walls of caves to scrolls to the Codex to what we know today as a book, covers thousands of years. Each of these advances in the art of writing had its skeptics who could not see the future implications. Can't you just hear the ancient monks talking about the difficulties of reading a codex instead of a scroll? However, I doubt if there are many Christian educators or pastors who have not relied heavily on reading and using books in their ministries. Every year billions of dollars are spent on Bibles, Sunday school curriculum, and worship bulletins. Where would we be without books to read?

Let me ask that question another way. Where will we be without books to play? That's right. We are entering an age in which the average child born in the year 2005 will grow up playing, not reading, a book. Instead of going to Barnes and Noble to purchase a book, they will download the books of their choice to their private book players.

In the July 1998 edition, *Wired* magazine reported that in the fall of that year, three digital book players would be released—Rocketbook, Softbook, and Everybook.[14] The long-term intent of these new toys is to replace the bound, paper and ink book. A new online company, NuvoMedia,[15] is supplying the digital books to be downloaded. Can Amazon.com and Barnes and Noble be far behind?

Sure, these first digital books are loaded with problems—from being too heavy to having only a limited number of available books. In the same way, when the Gutenberg Bible appeared in 1455 very few people knew how to read, the price of a book was prohibitive to most people, and the number of books was extremely limited.

There are those who argue that Martin Luther and the Protestant revolution could not have taken place had it not been for the printing press. Although this is not entirely valid, the press and the already wide distribution of books and other printed matter in Luther's time certainly added to the distribution of his ideas and work.

The opportunities afforded by e-books will be as far-reaching as those presented by the Gutenberg Bible. The difference is that whereas it took the printed book several hundred years to advance to where it is today, it will take the digital book no more than twenty years to rival the printed book.

Think of the implications: no more wasted paper, no more large boxes delivered to your door, no more need

for bulky bookshelves that take up space, no more waiting for a delivery that should have arrived yesterday,
interlink capabilities to other sources for those who wish
to go deeper, videos that jump out of the digital page, and
the ability to take several books along on vacation or
business.

I can hear the gasps again, "You can't take a good computer to bed with you!" It's only natural for people to
feel more comfortable with familiar things. However,
digital books will be cheaper than books and much
lighter. Video walls and video ceilings will also make
night reading much more enjoyable. You will actually
read lying down without your arms getting tired.

MegaClues for the Local Church

**1. Religious pluralism will flourish but ecu-
menism will fight an increasingly losing battle.**
Healthy churches are already crossing denominational
lines to work with churches of other denominations with
whom they have missional affinity. These congregations
work together around a common mission with little
regard for theological differences. At the same time,
those leaders interested in hammering out ecumenical
relationships based on a common theology are already
seeing the futility of their efforts. Healthy leaders are not
interested in getting denominations back together in one
big happy family. Instead, they are advancing the kin-
dom by getting multiple denominations to work together
around a mission too big for one denomination to achieve
on its own.

**2. The sharpest contrast between thriving and
dying churches continues to be a commitment to
Jesus Christ, indigenous styles of worship, and lay
ministries.**[16]
These will remain the "big three" in healthy congrega-

tions because they are the essence of the missional church.

3. High-commitment churches will have a better chance of reaching nonbelievers than low-commitment churches.[17]

A trend is already developing in fast-growing churches—the more requirements they place on membership, the more attendance grows. Those who never join have access to everything a member would have access to in a modern church.

The number of deeply committed Christians will become more numerous while nominal, cultural church members will continue to decrease. I see no evidence that the pre-Christian person will simply go through the motions of "going to church" like many church members during the last fifty years of Modernity.

4. Worship will continue to become more Eastern, ancient, and high-tech.

The issue is no longer contemporary versus traditional worship. Spirited traditional worship is growing churches and making disciples.[18] The key for the church on the OtherSide is whether or not it is "spirited." Does it have the mystery of the East, the integrity of the ancient, and the high tech of the West? Does it cause the hairs on the back of our necks to stand up? Does it stimulate hearts and challenge minds? Or do we continue to pray that Aunt Suzie does not die during worship while playing the organ?[19]

5. The majority of Protestant pastors could be women and the majority of Catholic churches could be run by deacons and women religious.

We are already seeing Protestant seminar enrollment reflect the growing role of women. More women religious are running Catholic churches. We will begin to see many of the clues in this book come to the front as women balance the emotional and cognitive aspects of leadership and lead in an intuitive and organic manner.[20]

6. Most of the effective pastors will receive their seminary training in a local church.

We are entering a time when the emphasis upon denominationally accredited professionals is being replaced by an emphasis on people with personal authenticity, spiritual integrity, and effective leadership. We are reverting to a time when laity were the ministers of the church and clergy had not been to seminary.[21]

Independent churches have been doing this for decades. Now more mainline churches are avoiding the seminary-trained graduate. They are developing farm systems within their churches. Ginghamsburg United Methodist Church reached an agreement with its bishop to allow them to train and empower "licensed pastors"—lay pastors to perform funerals, weddings, and baptisms.[22] I heard Lyle Schaller say at a Leadership Network event that churches should begin developing staff members as early as junior high.[23]

7. Church planting will be a primary mission of thriving, local church, and denominational systems.

A swell is already developing among church planting groups and coaches.[24] More and more local congregations are taking on the role of planting churches instead of waiting for their denomination. More and more new churches strive to plant a new church within the first five years of their lives. Church-planting resources are multiplying rapidly. Three things are driving this trend: (1) it is biblical; (2) most churches in the United States are located in the wrong place today (the people have moved); (3) it is easier to grow a new church than to transition a dying one.

8. Most ministry will be done by the congregation.

At the dawn of the pre-Christian world, pastoral and lay leadership are undergoing radical change. Pastoral leadership is equipping the congregation to live out their gifts. Leaders are guides and explorers forging a new set of rules for living by growing disciples who grow other disciples. The congregation is now out in the world representing God and growing disciples. Along with this trend, we will also see a gradual disappearance of the clergy/laity distinctions.

MegaClues for the Church at Large

1. Cyberchurches will become some of the largest churches and may be the new form of megachurch.[25]

The electronic church is already with us. The rapid growth of e-mail and the Internet is unprecedented in history. There is no way to deny the cyberchurch its place in the sun.

Those who say that the cyberchurch is not authentic because it cannot offer valid community simply have not been part of a cybercommunity. We have watched our online forums plan face-to-face meetings on numerous occasions. Those who refuse to see the authenticity of the electronic church are no different from those who said that the printed Bible would never catch on because people could not read.

2. Mainline denominations will never become multicultural in spite of their resolutions and affirmative action.

As long as denominations remain dominated by European forms of worship, they will never develop multicultural congregations. European forms of worship are so foreign to most cultures that they are one of the primary barriers to multicultural congregations. Most of the boats no longer come to the United States from Europe. Pentecostal congregations have long been multicultural because their worship style is close to the basic language of the world—rock and roll.

3. Social ministries will flourish as government continues to fail to meet social needs.

The government has come to the realization that it cannot provide everything that society needs. We will see it pull away from social services more and more. It will offer more funds to groups willing to provide basic services and it will tie less and less strings to those funds. Just about every social service, including Social Security, will be out of the hands of the government by the midpoint of the twenty-first century. This abandonment of people will leave a vast hole into which our churches can step and again become the primary educators and service providers.[26]

4. Worship is moving from an emphasis on music to visualization.

The arts are vital to the worship experience. Pre-Christian churches are taking on the characteristics of a gallery that includes great pieces of art from every recorded period in history. Spectacle and meditation are replacing reverence and praise. Ancient and future are merging. Secular and religious are blurring. Preaching is more "question and answer" and conversation than oratory. Everyday food and drink are becoming part of the liturgy. Mystery is back. Incense is in. Sarcasm is okay.

I won't be surprised if multiple images replace music as the primary form of worship for the pre-Christian—something like MTV on fast-forward with the sound turned down. In such a format, music becomes the backdrop for the constantly changing images. One hint from the past that suggests this might be a possibility is the fact that the images used on many music videos have little or nothing to do with the theme of the song.

5. Holographic imagery will form the basis for much of worship.

Several years ago at a national workshop at Ginghamsburg United Methodist Church in Tipp City, Ohio, I mentioned the use of holograms in worship. I mentioned it there because Ginghamsburg had just made a large financial commitment to reach the unchurched through multimedia. Tom Bandy and I wrote about the use of holographic imagery in worship in our recent book *Growing Spiritual Redwoods.* We called this church *The Virtual Church of the Resurrection.*[27] Aside from the usual funny looks, people always respond that the cost of such media is too high. My response is to ask them a question, "Do you have a pipe organ in your church? If so, then what I am talking about will be much less expensive than a pipe organ. It's just a matter of priorities."

Well, the future is now. The goal of Zebra Imaging in Austin, Texas, is "to put the ability to make holograms in the hands of the public."[28] The first desktop models for holographic imagery should be available by 2001. In a few short years the cost will plummet just as it has with personal computers.

If these issues bother you, it is only because you are not far enough through the wormhole. On the OtherSide, they will appear as normal as the telephone.

Is the Ride Over Yet?

Not on your life. For those wishing to continue the journey, go to **www.easumbandy.com/OtherSide** and explore the possibilities.

Over time, many of your reading companions will join you. I will be there also, lurking in the background. Now and then I will comment on the issues being shared. Feel free to make comments that will contribute to the ongoing learning process of leadership.

JOURNAL ENTRIES AND OTHER PAINFULLY WONDERFUL EXPERIENCES TO HELP YOU FEEL AND THINK

1. Which of the MegaClues will most affect you, your church, and your world?

2. Which of the MegaClues do you hope will not come true?

3. If your church does not have a web page, why not ask some teenagers to design one for you. This would be a good intergenerational endeavor.

4. Spend time designing your church's technology plan for the future. How will it be affected by your facilities? Will they be able to handle it? How will the technology enhance the mission of your church? What equipment will you need?

5. Purchase a copy of *Creature III* and explore with your child or children the differences between how easily they can create and nurture online compared to how difficult it is for you. Have fun on their website at **www.creatures.mindscape. com**.

6. For more on the forces shaping our society see my book *Dancing with Dinosaurs*, pages 13-14 and 25-33. All the issues explored in those pages are still as relevant as ever.

Notes

Introduction: Leadership on the OtherSide

1. See Peter M. Senge, *The Fifth Discipline: The Art and Practice of the Learning Organization* (New York: Doubleday, 1994). Senge calls these "mental models." I don't like "mental model" for two reasons: (1) the word "mental" sounds too rational, and (2) the word "model" feels too static and mechanical.

2. For a brief explanation of spiritual gifts, see my book *Sacred Cows Make Gourmet Burgers: Ministry Anytime, Anywhere, by Anyone* (Nashville: Abingdon Press, 1995). Also, to take a free short online inventory to discover your gifts, see **http://www.cforce.com/sgifts.cgi** and **http://www.joyriver.org/church/ministries/inventory-a.html**.

3. For more on quantum mechanics, see **http://newton/ex.ac.uk/people/jenkins/mbody/mbody2.html** or **http://www-wilson.ucsd.edu/education/qm/qm/html**.

4. If after you have finished the book you find yourself wishing that I had given more concrete examples of the type of leadership it will take in the new world, then work on your ability to dream and imagine.

5. For a brief explanation of the different ways of referring to postmodernism, see Steven Best and Douglas Kellner, *The Postmodern Turn* (New York: Guilford Press, 1997).

6. See Laurie Beth Jones, *The Path: Creating Your Mission Statement for Work and for Life* (New York: Hyperion, 1996).

1. The Challenge of Our Times

1. Christendom began sometime between A.D. 312 and 327 when Flavius Valerius Constantinus, better known as Constantine the Great, adopted Christianity as the favored religion of the Roman Empire. When Christendom came to an end is more difficult to pinpoint. Most likely it happened sometime between World War II and the 1980s. During its time, Christianity was the dominant religion of the Western world.

2. See **http://www.americanwholehealth.com/library/acupuncture/ylnyang.htm**.

3. See Acts 6 where the twelve refuse to allow such ministries to take time away from God's calling to disciple people to make disciples of Jesus Christ.

4. "The gifts he gave were that some would be apostles, some prophets, some evangelists, some pastors and teachers, to equip the saints for the work of ministry, for building up the body of Christ" (Ephesians 4:11-12).

5. Copyright © January 1999 by Brad Sargent. Used by permission.

6. In systems theory, this is called homeostasis.

7. According to systems theory, there are two orders of change—first and second order. First-order change does not change the entire system, only a part of it. Second-order change changes the system. For this to happen, our Life Metaphors must change. For a detailed analysis of systems theory and various types of loopiness, see Peter M. Senge, *The Fifth Discipline: The Art and Practice of the Learning Organization* (New York: Doubleday, 1994).

8. Two books have had a profound influence on my understanding of leadership. The first is *The Human Side of Leadership* by Douglas McGregor (New York: McGraw-Hill, 1960). The original is out of print, but there is a twenty-fifth anniversary printing that is still available. In the 1960 original, he wrote about the theory of X and Y. The management style of theory X is that people are basically lazy and need to be coerced or manipulated into working. Theory Y describes the kind of manager who believes that people want to work and be productive, and the manager's role is to remove the obstacles. Theory Y describes a leader who creates an environment in which people are free to live out their spiritual gifts without having to ask some board or agency for permission. For a closer look at his theory, see **http://www.sundial.net/ ~RussRP.html**.

Next, is Robert Greenleaf's book *Soul Leadership* (Mahwah, N.J.: Paulist Press, 1977). Greenleaf wrote that true servant leadership causes others to "grow as persons [and] while being served, become healthier, wiser, freer, more autonomous, and more likely themselves to become servants" (p. 241). I can think of no greater joy as a leader.

9. Daniel Goleman, *Emotional Intelligence: Why It Can Matter More Than IQ* (New York: Bantam, 1997).

2. Into the Wormhole

1. For a mind-blowing discussion of the changes occurring today read Willis Harman, *Global Mind Change* (San Francisco: Berrett-Koehler, 1998). See also **http://www.noetic.org**.

2. For an interesting site on wormholes, see **http://www.netlabs.net/ hp/tremor/wormholes.html**. To see several sites go to **http://www.dogpile.com** and search for wormholes, then click on the wormholes and you will get the top ten visited websites on wormholes. If you want to have some fun with the wormhole, go to **http://www.geocities.com/Area51/Nebula/964/index.html**.

3. For more on the speed of age, see James D. Davidson and Rees Mogg, *The Sovereign Individual: How to Survive and Thrive During the Collapse of the Welfare State* (New York: Simon & Schuster, 1997).

4. For more on blur, see Stan Davis and Christopher Meyer, *Blur: The Speed of Change in the Connected Economy* (Reading, Mass.: Addison-Wesley, 1998).

5. Because we have the tools to record and reflect on the changes, we

are the first generation of people to realize that they are passing from one epoch to another. If we fail to see what is happening, it is simply because we choose not to see.

6. Willis Harman, *Global Mind Change*, p. 194.

7. Kevin Kelly, *New Rules for the New Economy* (New York: Viking, 1998).

8. For more on chaos theory, read James Gleick, *Chaos: Making a New Science* (New York: Penguin, 1988) or Margaret J. Wheatley, *Leadership and the New Science: Learning About Organization from an Orderly Universe* (San Francisco: Berrett-Koehler, 1999). For those wishing to go deeper, see M. Mitchell Waldrop, *Complexity: The Emerging Science at the Edge of Order and Chaos* (New York: Touchstone Books, 1993). For an in-depth article on chaos theory, as well as interesting graphics, see **http://www.iglobal.net/pub/camelot/chaos/chaos.htm**.

9. Probably at this point some theologians are wincing at my theology, but who cares if it brings order out of chaos. All I can say is, "Get over it."

10. See the William C. Creasy translation of *The Imitation of Christ* by Thomas à Kempis (Notre Dame, Ind.: Ave Maria Press, 1989).

11. We are seeing this doubling-back effect in worship as more and more pre-Christian churches are using ancient forms of music such as Gregorian chant. It is called "the Gorecki Phenomenon." See **http://www. regenerator.com/contents.html**. Go to volume 4, number 2, with the baby's picture on it.

12. Leonard Sweet, *SoulTsunami* (Grand Rapids: Zondervan, 1999).

13. An interesting book on creativity is Alan G. Robinson and Sam Stern, *Corporation Creativity: How Innovation and Improvement Actually Happen* (San Francisco: Berrett-Koehler, 1997).

14. For more, see Charles W. Prather and Lisa Gundry, *Blueprints for Innovation* (New York: AMACOM, 1995).

15. William Easum, *The Church Growth Handbook* (Nashville: Abingdon Press, 1990).

16. Randall P. White, Phil Hodgson, and Stuart Crainer, *The Future of Leadership: Riding the Corporate Rapids into the 21st Century* (London: Pitman Medical, 1996).

17. See Malibu Vineyard, **http://www.malibuvineyard.org**; Coast Hills Church, **http://www.coasthillschurch.org**; and **http://www2.christianity.net/ct/7TD/7TD055.html**. For an article on how churches are using the arts see **http://www.worship.org/Article.asp?ArticleID=52&Volume=7**.

18. One of the most important books of the last decade is Gareth Morgan's *Images of Organization: The Executive Edition* (San Francisco: Berrett-Koehler, 1998).

19. For those wanting more, see Lewis Mumford, *The Transformation of Man* (New York: Harper Brothers, 1956).

20. William Bridges, *Managing Transition: Making the Most of Change* (Portland, Oreg.: Perseus Press, 1991).

21. Leonard Sweet, *SoulTsunami*, p. 77.

3. The Death of Two Kissing Cousins

1. For the definition of Modernity found in the *Oxford Dictionary of Literary Terms*, see **http://virtual.park.uga.edu/~232/voc/**

modernism.voc.html. For a more comprehensive look, albeit biased, see **http://www.modcult.brown.edu/people/scholes/modlist/title.html**. For a comprehensive timeline of Modernity see **http://faculty. washington.edu/eckman/timeline.html**. This last website will allow you to make suggestions as to what has been left out of the timeline.

2. Ken Wilber, *The Marriage of Sense and Soul: Integrating Science and Religion* (New York: Broadway, 1999).

3. The battle between science and religion is giving way to a marriage between science and religion. Dean Overman in his article "Not a Chance" says that the possibility that life just happened is problematic due to almost impossible odds of the right combination of amino acids joining together in just the right amount at just the right time to form even short proteins, much less the DNA found in life. Dean Overman, "Not a Chance," *American Enterprise* 9 (September/October 1998): 34-37.

4. For an interesting time, see **http://www.skeptic.com**.

5. For a discussion of the effects of quantum physics, see chapter 2 of my book *Sacred Cows Make Gourmet Burgers* (Nashville: Abingdon Press, 1995).

6. For the ten most visited websites on quantum mechanics go to **http://www.dogpile.com** and search for quantum mechanics.

7. William Easum, *Dancing with Dinosaurs: Ministry in a Hostile and Hurting World* (Nashville: Abingdon Press, 1993), p. 23.

8. For a fuller description, see William M. Easum and Thomas G. Bandy, *Growing Spiritual Redwoods* (Nashville: Abingdon Press, 1997).

9. Ibid., p. 22.

10. G. W. F. Hegel and evangelical Donald Bloesch argue that postmodernism is not really a successor to modernism but a reaction *within* the overarching category of modernism, not unlike romanticism, which reacted to many of the same excesses of modernism and shares many, though not all, of the characteristics of postmodernism. If the problem of contemporary culture is simply that it has failed to adjust to change, then Hegel and Bloesch are correct in saying that postmodernism is but a romantic corrective within modernism itself, and that eventually a higher synthesis will emerge. There is no radical break with modernism, only the eternal pattern. On the other hand, if the problem with modern culture is not merely that it has failed to adjust, but that there are fundamental assumptions within modernism that are essentially wrong, then the postmodern period is a revolutionary break with modernism and a new template of understanding is required.

11. The entrance to the wormhole bears a remarkable resemblance to the world of the first-century church. The world into which Christianity was born was a cosmopolitan, diverse, patchwork quilt. Most of the population was gathered into large cities where they suffered from the problems customary to urban areas. The Roman Empire was characterized by a large disparity in income and living conditions.

The Empire was also riddled with a myriad of religions and superstitions. As Rome conquered, it also included the gods of the region into its pantheon of gods. The early Christians found themselves confronting many forms of oriental cults on the outside and gnostic heresy on the inside. A profound fatalism filled the lives of most people. Belief in cult powers, like our reliance on psychic 1-900 telephone lines, left the people with a sense of futility.

To reach such a world, the early Christians had to be, on the one hand, extremely flexible and diverse in the ways they responded to the challenges and, on the other hand, extremely firm in their belief system. The world was floundering in superstition and fatalism. The "no fear" of today could be seen on the faces of the average person in the Empire. To respond to their needs the early Christians had to offer an infallible revelation in Jesus Christ that offered a clear meaning of life and the hope of overcoming the malign forces that threatened to engulf the people. For more on the world into which Christianity was born, see E. Glenn Hinson, *The Early Church: Origins to the Dawn of the Middle Ages* (Nashville: Abingdon Press, 1996).

12. One of the best ways to get a flavor for this world is to read from the writings of the first and second century. A simple place to begin is at one of the following: **http://www.iclnet.org/pub/resources/ christian-history.html#fathers, http://wesley.nnc.edu/noncanon/ fathers.htm**, or **http://www.ccel.wheaton.edu/fathers2**.

13. For more on the impact of divorce on children, go to **http://www. dogpile.com** and search for divorce, then click on "impact of divorce on children."

14. For more on how to be a radical Christian without being a bigot, see William M. Easum and Thomas G. Bandy, *Growing Spiritual Redwoods,* pp. 53-65.

15. The word used to describe them is "apologists" (apology means to make a defense). The most famous are Justin Martyr, Perpetua, Irenaeus, Tertullian, Origen, and Augustine. The apologists defended Christianity not only against paganism from the outside but also from heresy within. Justin Martyr defended the faith from the charges of Romans and Jews, and Irenaeus defended the faith against the Gnostics who threatened Christianity from within. For more, see **http://ccat.sas.upenn.edu/~humm/Resources/Bauer/bauer06.htm**.

16. Gnosticism was based on the radical dualism of spirit and matter. Spirit was good and matter was evil, therefore God could not have created the world and Jesus could not have been human. Irenaeus was the primary apologist to take on this view. He argued that the God of creation was also the God of salvation and that Jesus was both divine and human. For more, see Irenaeus, *The Treatise of Irenaeus of Lugdunum Against the Heresies,* trans. and ed. F. R. Montgomery Hitchcock (London: Society for Promoting Christian Knowledge, 1916), pp. 84-89 and 67-68. For more on Gnosticism see the following:

> **http://www.themystica.com/mystica/articles/m/magus_simon.htm**
> **http://www.themystica.com/mystica/articles/g/gnosticism.html**
> **http://www.talkcity.com/calendar/category/spirituality2.html**

In the third century, Origen was the first to develop a systematic approach to the faith beyond the apostolic tradition. His work is called "On First Principles." This was a textbook of instructions covering numerous issues relating to creation, the nature of humanity, good and evil, and the way of salvation, which centered in Jesus Christ. Later, Origen came under suspicion of heretical tendencies and lost some credibility, but still, he was one of the first for his time to take a stab at an apologetic.

In the fourth century, Augustine set the standards in his work, for all future apologetics. For reviews of some of the best of Augustine's work, see **http://www.iclnet.org/pub/resources/christian-history. html#fathers**.

17. Michael Slaughter's book *Spiritual Entrepreneurs: Six Principles for Risking Renewal* (Nashville: Abingdon Press, 1995) focuses on the spiritual qualifications of leadership. The book shares the type of spirituality that enabled Michael to lead Ginghamsburg United Methodist Church from being a tiny country church of ninety people to being a church with over 3,000 in worship even though it is located in open countryside. The book offers no gimmicks, just six segments of theology.

18. My guess is that such an apologetic will lean heavily on art and poetry.

4. The Mother Life Metaphor

1. Frank B. Copley, *Frederick B. Taylor: Father of Scientific Management, Vol. 1* (New York: Kelley, 1969), pp. 356-57.

2. In his book *Brave New World* (Madison, Wis.: Demco, 1969), Aldous Huxley adopted a new dating system, "B.F." and "A.F.," meaning "Before Ford" and "After Ford."

3. I made this mistake in my first book, *The Church Growth Handbook* (Nashville: Abingdon Press, 1990).

4. Deepak Chopra, *Seven Spiritual Laws of Success: A Practical Guide to the Fulfillment of Your Dreams* (San Rafael, Calif.: Amber-Allen, 1994), p. 53.

5. Margaret J. Wheatley and Myron Kellner-Rogers, *A Simpler Way* (San Francisco: Berrett-Koehler, 1999).

6. The DNA itself codes these characteristics by a series of protein bases arranged on a spiral sugar ladder. Many of the characteristics are hidden or blended when the two gametes come together so that the resultant characteristics of a distinct individual are formed. After the birth of the individual the DNA continues to work through various types of RNA to run the organism and develop the various physical, mental, emotional, and operational characteristics interacting with the external environment. For a picture of DNA, see **http://www.easumbandy.com/OtherSide.**

7. One of the best selling books on the relationship of organisms to organizations is Margaret J. Wheatley, *Leadership and the New Science* (San Francisco: Barrett-Koehler, 1999). For a brief summary of the book, see **http://www.kaneandassociates.com/summary2.htm**.

8. In our book *Growing Spiritual Redwoods* (Nashville: Abingdon Press, 1997), Tom Bandy and I referred to DNA as the mission statement and the genes as the vision, values, and belief statements.

9. For more information, see **http://www.easumbandy.com/faqs/mission-statement.htm**.

10. William M. Easum and Thomas G. Bandy, *Growing Spiritual Redwoods.*

11. Kenneth H. Blanchard, *Managing By Values* (San Francisco: Berrett-Koehler, 1997).

12. Rick Warren, *The Purpose Driven Church* (Grand Rapids: Zondervan, 1996).

13. Aubrey Malphurs, *Values Driven Leadership: Discovering and Developing Your Core Values for Ministry* (Grand Rapids: Baker Books, 1996).

14. In *Growing Spiritual Redwoods,* Tom Bandy and I referred to these

as the "Mission Statement" (Why), "Vision Statement" (How), and "Values Statement" (What). I have chosen to refer to them as "Why," "How," and "What" because of the confusion these terms seem to raise among church leaders. Too many people interchange the use of "vision" and "mission." Others confuse "vision" and "vision casting" (their preferred future) with "Vision Statements."

15. For several examples, see our website **http://www.easumbandy.com/faqs/mission-statements.htm**.

16. See **http://www.easumbandy.com/others/Morris.htm** for an article by Danny Morris that explains how to turn the Nominating Committee into a discerning body.

17. For more, see William M. Easum, *Sacred Cows Make Gourmet Burgers* (Nashville: Abingdon Press, 1995).

18. For more, see Peter Senge, *The Fifth Discipline: The Art and Practice of the Learning Organization* (New York: Doubleday, 1994). For a wonderful book that explains the importance of embedding DNA in leadership, see Margaret J. Wheatley and Myron Kellner-Rogers, *A Simpler Way*.

19. That's one reason God asks us to set aside a day a week to remember who we are and why we are here. The children of Israel in the wilderness repeatedly asked Moses why he had brought them out into the wilderness to die when there were plenty of graves in Egypt. Nehemiah found that every twenty-one days he had to remind people why they were building the wall. I remember seeing a study years ago that showed people made or broke a habit every twenty-one days.

20. For information on how various churches have developed their DNA see **http://www.easumbandy.com/OtherSide**.

21. I am indebted here to the following churches for the opportunity to consult with them and learn from them: Ginghamsburg United Methodist Church in Tipp City, Ohio; New Hope Christian Fellowship (Foursquare Gospel) in Honolulu, Hawaii; Prince of Peace Lutheran Church in Burnsville, Minnesota; and Christ United Methodist Church in Fort Lauderdale, Florida.

22. Learned during a church consultation with Christ Church in 1997.

23. From an interview with Michael Slaughter in early 1998.

24. To learn more about the journey of Dick Wills and his congregation see Dick Wills, *Waking to God's Dream: Spiritual Leadership and Church Renewal* (Nashville: Abingdon Press, 1999).

25. For more on spiritual gifts, see William M. Easum, *Sacred Cows Make Gourmet Burgers*. For an online free version see **http://www.cforc.com/sgifts.cgi** or **http://ftp.elca.org/eteam/assessment/opening.htm**.

26. Robert Greenleaf, *The Servant as Leader* (Indianapolis: The Greenleaf Center, 1970), p. 7.

27. I have seen several methods of fractalling, such as the *Cell Church Model* and *Cell Net*, a networking of cell-based congregations by Touch Ministries in Houston, Texas. Another is Ralph Neighbor's group, about which you can learn by calling 1-713-497-7901. There is a cell church BBS on the Internet that can be accessed through America Online. It is called "Cell-Church." **Listserv@Bible.ACU.EDU**.

Cell Track is a software package for keeping track of small groups and all that goes with them. For information, call 1-800-735-5865. *Cell*

Church magazine is a helpful publication. Contact them at 14925 Memorial Drive, Suite 101, Houston, Texas 77079. Phone 1-713-497-7901.

The *Groups of Twelve* that originated in Brazil is now being tested in the United States by Bethany World Center, Baker, Louisiana, and by the Church of the Nations, Athens, Georgia.

Another example is the *Meta Small Group Model.* New Hope Community Church is the largest example of this model in North America. Other examples are Cornerstone Church in Harrisonburg, Virginia; Ginghamsburg Church in Tipp City, Ohio; and Willow Creek Church in South Burnsville, Illinois. For more see the *Small Group Network* on the Internet. It has a wonderful array of resources. See **http://www.smallgroups.com**.

28. For more, see Wayne Cordeiro, *Doing Church as a Team* (Honolulu: ICM Press, 1998). ICM Press is at New Hope Christian Fellowship, Box 11132, Honolulu, Hawaii 96828. See also **http://www.New Hope-hawaii.org**.

29. Chaos theory is one of the new illustrations of hope. For more on the relationship of chaos to Christian ministry, see Thomas Bandy, *Christian Chaos: Revolutionizing the Congregation* (Nashville: Abingdon Press, 1999).

30. For more on horizontal promotions, see Bruce Tulgan, *The Pocket Manager's Guide to Generation X* (Amherst, Mass.: HRD Press, 1997).

31. For more on class meetings, see D. Michael Henderson, *John Wesley's Class Meeting: A Model for Making Disciples* (Nappanee, Ind.: Evangel Publishing House, 1997).

5. Spiritual Guides: Explorers of the OtherSide

1. Ada Maria Isasi-Diaz, an ethnicist at Drew University, uses the term "kin-dom," rather than "kingdom."

2. Many churches are now so old that the facilities are beginning to require more and more upkeep. Many churches spend 35 to 40 percent of the total income keeping their facilities from falling down. This amount is three to four times what the average church in the United States gives to missions. For more information, see M. D. Wilcox, "On a Shoestring and a Prayer," *Kiplinger's Personal Finance* 53 (May 1999): 96-101.

3. "The God Movement" was Clarence Jordan's translation of the word "gospel" in his *Cotton Patch Version* of the New Testament. See *The Cotton Patch Version of Luke and Acts* (New York: Association Press, 1969) and *The Cotton Patch Version of Matthew and John* (New York: Association Press, 1970).

4. Rudolf Bultmann's school of thought believes that the truth in the Bible is a mixture of culture (religious myth) and divine truth. The cultural aspects (the vehicles used to convey the truth) must be stripped away, "demythologized," to the truth. The reader must look beyond the historical record to find the real message.

5. For information on alternate and holistic health care, see **http://www.opencenter.org** or **http://www.esalen.org.education**.

6. As of this writing, an Alta Vista search for "home schooling" and "charter schooling" reveals more than 7,000 and 8,000 sites respectively.

7. The three most dramatic examples of community are the Internet, cohousing, and house churches. The Internet communities include more than 420,000 sites. One of the best chat sites is **http://www. talkcity.com**. There is one site for spirituality that covers "Christian, JesusCafe, Reflecting Pool, and Women-spiritual." To see an example of cohousing go to **http://web.mit.edu/jenise/www/cstone/ cstone.html**. There are more than 1,900 sites for house churches. See **http://www.hccentral.com/cgi/redirect.cgi?file=flinks. html**.

8. See Alan Briskin, *The Stirring of Soul in the Workplace* (San Francisco: Jossey-Bass, 1996); Charles Kiefer and Peter Senge, *Transforming Work* (Alexandria, Va.: Miles River Press, 1998); and the many books by Robert Greenleaf on servant leadership. See **http://www.greenleaf.org**.

9. To name a few examples: John Barrow and Frank Tippler, *The Anthropic Cosmological Principle* (Oxford: Oxford University Press, 1990); the many books by John C. Polkinghorne, but especially *Belief in God in an Age of Science* (New Haven: Yale University Press, 1998); G. Scott Sparrow, *I Am with You Always: True Stories of Encounters with Jesus* (New York: Bantam, 1995); and Andrew Greely, *The Sociology of the Paranormal: A Reconnaissance* (Beverly Hills, Calif.: Sage Publications, 1975).

10. Several Protestant offerings can be found: Academies of Spiritual Direction, The United Methodist Church, and Shalem Institute in Washington, D.C. There is an article describing spiritual direction from the Shalem Institute. Their website is **http://www.shalem.org/sd.html**. The Presbyterian San Francisco Theological Seminary has a program called the Program for Christian Spirituality.

11. Morton T. Kelsey, *Companions on the Inner Way: The Art of Spiritual Guidance* (New York: Crossroad Publishing, 1995), p. 7.

12. Ignatius of Loyola spent all his life working on "The Spiritual Exercises," a book which 350 years later is still the standard for spiritual direction for individuals. Anthony Mottola trans., *The Spiritual Exercises of St. Ignatius* (New York: Doubleday, 1964).

13. One of the best quick reads on the subject of spiritual direction is William A. Barry, *The Practice of Spiritual Direction* (San Francisco: HarperSanFrancisco, 1986). Or read Morton T. Kelsey, *Companions on the Inner Way*. For a deeper look at the many varieties of spiritual direction see David L. Fleming, "Models of Spiritual Direction," *Review for the Religious* 34 (1974): 351-57.

14. Jane Kise, *Lifekeys: Discovering Who You Are, Why You Are Here, What You Do Best* (Minneapolis: Bethany House, 1996).

15. Danny E. Morris and Charles M. Olsen, *Discerning God's Will Together: A Spiritual Practice for the Church* (Bethesda: Alban Institute, 1997). For an article on this subject, see **http://www. easumbandy.com/OtherSide/OtherSide.htm**.

16. What would Jesus do?

17. Local church example: Fellowship Bible Church in Little Rock, Arkansas, **http://www.fellowshipnwa.org**. City Reach examples: International Urban Associates led by Ray Bakke

http://www.cl.ais.net/iua1/. For an in-depth article on IUA and Ray Bakke on this site, see Curtis Sittenfield, "The Real Challenge Facing the World Is Not Geographical Distance but Cultural Distance." You can also subscribe free to a newsletter called *City Voices*, put out by International Urban Associates.

For an article on Ray Bakke, see Curtis Sittenfield, "Social Justice—Ray Bakke," *Fast Company* 20 (December 1998): 168 at **http://www. fastcompany.com/pnline/20/bakke.html**.

Other examples include *Vision New England* at **http:// www.vision4ne.org**, led by Steve Machia; *Mission Houston,* led by Jim Herrington; and the *Harambee Christian Family Center* in Los Angeles, led by Rudy Carrasco, **http://www.harambee.org**. For a fascinating article on partnerships, see **http://www.leadnet.org/leadnet/ index2.html**.

18. If MUDs (multiuser domains) are new to you, go to **http://www. dogpile.com** and search for MUDs. You will find a list of sites that gives the basics and you will also get a list of the most popular sites. I have found that many of the sites no longer work, so you will have to poke around.

6. The Lone Ranger Was a Team Player

1. See Jay A. Conger, Gretchen M. Spreitzer, Edward E. Lawler III, eds., *The Leader's Change Handbook: An Essential Guide to Setting Direction and Taking Action* (San Francisco: Jossey-Bass, 1998) for articles from people such as Michael Beer, Thomas Cummings, and Susan Mohrman.

For a great article on the myths surrounding the heroic leader, download "Ten Myths About Post-Heroic Leadership—And Why They Are Wrong" by David Stauffer at **http://www.hbsp.harvard.edu/ hbsp/prod_detail.asp?U9804A**.

2. William M. Easum and Thomas G. Bandy, *Growing Spiritual Redwoods* (Nashville: Abingdon Press, 1997), pp. 183-202.

3. Roberta Hestenes, *Turning Committees into Communities* (Colorado Springs: Navpress, 1991).

4. *Building Teams for Twenty-first Century Ministry (7023).* To order the tape go to **http://www.fuller.edu/cee/html/pastupdt.html**.

5. William M. Easum, *How to Reach Baby Boomers* (Nashville: Abingdon Press, 1991).

6. For information on how to deal with controllers, see William M. Easum, *Sacred Cows Make Gourmet Burgers* (Nashville: Abingdon Press, 1995), pp. 31-38. Be prepared—many people do not like this section of the book. It strikes too close to home.

7. For a brief list of some permission-giving churches, see **http://www.easumbandy.com/faqs/permissiongivingchurches.html**.

8. I first developed this concept in my book *Sacred Cows Make Gourmet Burgers.*

9. The story of Dick Wills and Christ Church can be found in Dick Wills, *Waking to God's Dream: Spiritual Leadership and Church Renewal* (Nashville: Abingdon Press, 1999). You can visit their website at **http://www.christchurchum.org**.

10. For an interview of Bill Easum by *Vital* magazine, see **http://www.easumbandy.com/permission/interview.htm**.

11. William M. Easum, *How to Reach Baby Boomers.*
12. For an example, see Acts 4.
13. For more information on teams, see **http://www.easum/ com/bybill/teams.htm.**
14. See **http://www.easumbandy.com/networksindex.htm.**
15. Here are two to explore: **http://www.firstcyberchurch.orgn/ evangelism** and **http://websyte.com/PositiveChurch.**
16. George Cladis, *Leading the Team-Based Church* (San Francisco: Jossey-Bass, 1999), pp. 5 and 9.
17. You will find a tool to help you determine the willingness of the people to make such a transition, and where to begin the process, in my book *Sacred Cows Make Gourmet Burgers,* pp. 170-72.

7. Whose Church Is It, Anyway?

1. For an excellent treatment of servanthood, see Douglas John Hall, *The Steward: A Biblical Symbol Come of Age* (Grand Rapids: Eerdmans, 1990).
2. To see a church where the laity marry and bury see Ginghamsburg United Methodist Church in Tipp City, Ohio. **http:// www.ginghamsburg.org**
3. For more on how to do this, see William M. Easum, *Sacred Cows Make Gourmet Burgers* (Nashville: Abingdon Press, 1995).
4. Instead of begging people to teach Sunday school, the church in which I served Christ for twenty-four years required people to take two hours of training each week for nine months before they could teach. As a result, we always had an abundance of teachers. It was a privilege reserved only for servants. Volunteers were turned off by this requirement.
5. In the Acts of the Apostles, new leaders were chosen by the existing leaders instead of by a congregational vote. See Acts 6 for one example.
6. I am not overlooking the fact that third-world leaders have their own problems. It's just that more and more of the ministries that are working well in the United States, such as small groups, lay pastors, high commitments, and fractalling are used extensively in third-world countries.
7. The midwife understanding of leadership eliminates any view of leadership that says that the primary role of leaders is to take care of the needs of the members of the church, or any view of leadership that includes a dictator.
8. Ronald Heifetz, "The Leader of the Future," *Fast Company* (June 1999): 132.
9. James M. Kouzes and Barry Z. Posner, *Encouraging the Heart: A Leader's Guide to Rewarding and Recognizing Others* (San Francisco: Jossey-Bass, 1999).
10. For more on systems and how to kick the habits that can kill churches, see Tom Bandy, *Kicking Habits: Welcome Relief for Addicted Churches* (Nashville: Abingdon Press, 1997).
11. He called them "white sepulchers" and by doing so attacked the very heart of their priesthood based on purity. Jesus loved church leaders too much to allow them to remain such small persons. When Peter

showed his displeasure over the impending death of his Lord, Jesus said to him, "Get thee behind me, Satan." Jesus loved his disciples too much to let them miss one of the more important lessons of servanthood. Jesus, the man who said, "be compassionate as God is compassionate," had no desire to be nice, because being nice has nothing to do with being a Christian.

8. Almost to the OtherSide

1. For more, see Don Tapscott, *Growing Up Digital: The Rise of the Net Generation* (New York: McGraw-Hill, 1997).

2. For more information, you can read Nicholas Negroponte, *Being Digital* (New York: Random House, 1996); Don Tapscott, *Growing Up Digital;* Kevin Kelly, *Out of Control: The New Biology of Machines, Social Systems, and the Economic World* (Reading, Mass.: Addison-Wesley, 1994); Leonard Sweet, *SoulTsunami* (Grand Rapids: Zondervan, 1999).

3. For more on the difference between information and data, see Clifford Stoll, *Silicon Snake Oil: Second Thoughts on the Information Highway* (New York: Doubleday, 1996).

4. For those wanting to know about nanotechnology, see **http://itri.loyola.edu/nanobase**. Also, **http://www.zyvex.com/nano**.

5. Bruce Mazlish, *The Fourth Discontinuity: The Co-evolution of Humans and Machines* (New Haven: Yale University Press, 1995). For more, see David Channell, *The Vital Machine: A Study in Technology and Organic Life* (New York: Oxford University Press, 1991).

6. Kevin Kelly, *Out of Control,* p. 109.

9. Remain Seated with Your Seat Belt Buckled: The Ride's Not Over

1. You can visit Mars Hill by going to **http://www.marshillchurch.org**.

2. You can subscribe free by going to **http://www.easumbandy.com/networksindex.htm** and subscribing. God go with you on your journey.

10. Welcome to the OtherSide

1. To see how this works or to order resources, go to **http://www.easumbandy.com**, then to resources, then to workbooks.

2. For more on house churches, see **http://www.hcentral.com**.

3. One of the best sites is **http://www.ginghamsburg.org**.

4. Those wanting to learn more about how to use the Internet may want to purchase a copy of *Harvard Business Review's Internet Strategy Handbook: Lessons From the New Frontier of Business* (New York: McGraw-Hill, 1996). A better way to stay current is to subscribe to either *Wired* magazine or *PC Computing*. For an interesting debate on the future of the Internet, go to **http://search.bt.com** and search for "future of Internet."

5. For more, read Willis Harman, *Global Mind Change* (San Francisco: Berrett-Koehler, 1998).

6. **http://www.bt.com**

7. **http://www.emory.edu**

8. **http://www.hnc.com**

9. Rosalind W. Picard, *Affective Computing* (Cambridge, Mass.: MIT Press, 1997).

10. William Easum, *Dancing with Dinosaurs* (Nashville: Abingdon Press, 1993), p. 26. See also Martin Marty, "A Special Issue: The Human Genome Project," *Context* 21 (1990): 3.

11. For more information see **http://www.edutainco.com**.

12. To enjoy *Sesame Street* online, see **http://www.ctw.org/sesame/0.1292.00.html**.

13. For more see Jim Krefft, "Designing for the Twenty-first Century," *Journal of Business Strategy* (November/December 1998). Krefft is from Six Sigma Qualtec, which is the twenty-first-century version of Total Quality Management.

14. To see how e-books work go to **http://www.rocket-ebook.com** or **http://www.softbook.com** or **http://www.everybk.com**.

15. For more information, see **http://www.Nuvomedia.com**.

16. For more information on indigenous worship, see William M. Easum and Thomas G. Bandy, *Growing Spiritual Redwoods* (Nashville: Abingdon Press, 1997), chapter 4.

17. High-commitment churches are those who focus on their DNA, are discipling people to follow Jesus, and have indigenous worship and groups.

18. One of the best examples of this is Church of the Resurrection United Methodist Church in Kansas City, Kansas. Go to www.cor.org.

19. The Church of the Resurrection United Methodist Church in Kansas City, Kansas, is a good example. See **http://www.cor.org**.

20. For examples of such leadership, see Sally Helgesen, *Female Advantage: Women's Ways of Leadership* (New York: Doubleday, 1995).

21. Prior to 1950 most pastors had not been to seminary.

22. **http://www.ginghamsburg.org**.

23. One of the best training groups in the United States is *Leadership Network*. You can find them at **http://www.leadnet.org**.

24. For more information, see *Church Multiplication Center* at **http://www.cmtcmultiply.org** and Jim Griffith at **http://www.griffithcoaching.com**.

25. Two examples of churches online are **http://www.cyberchurch.org** and **http://www.hawaiian.net/~mpilot**.

26. For more, see James D. Davidson and Rees Mogg, *The Sovereign Individual: How to Survive and Thrive During the Collapse of the Welfare State* (New York: Simon & Schuster, 1997).

27. William M. Easum and Thomas G. Bandy, *Growing Spiritual Redwoods*, pp. 90-93.

28. Mark Frauenfelder, "The Holo Trintity," *Wired* (July 1998): 7. See also **http://www.zebra.com**.

Bibliography

Bandy, Thomas G. *Moving Off the Map: A Field Guide to Changing the Congregation.* Nashville: Abingdon Press, 1998.

Barry, William A. *The Practice of Spiritual Direction.* San Francisco: HarperSanFrancisco, 1986.

Best, Stephen, and Douglas Kellner. *The Postmodern Turn.* New York: Guilford Press, 1997.

Blanchard, Carol and Randolph. *Empowerment Takes More Than a Minute.* San Francisco: Berrett-Koehler, 1996.

Blanchard, Kenneth. *Managing By Values.* San Francisco: Berrett-Koehler, 1994.

Borg, Martin. *Meeting Jesus Again for the First Time.* San Francisco: HarperSanFrancisco, 1994.

Bridges, William. *Managing Transition: Making the Most of Change.* Portland, Oreg.: Perseus Press, 1991.

Briskin, Alan. *The Stirring of the Soul in the Workplace.* San Francisco: Jossey-Bass, 1996.

Bruggeman, Walter. *Cadences of Home.* Louisville: Westminster John Knox, 1997.

Burns, MacGregor. *Leadership.* New York: Harper & Row, 1978.

Channell, David. *The Vital Machine: A Study in Technology and Organic Life.* New York: Oxford University Press, 1991.

Chopra, Deepak. *The Seven Spiritual Laws of Success: A Practical Guide to the Fulfillment of Your Dreams.* San Rafael: Calif.: Amber-Allen, 1994.

Conger, Jay A., Gretchen M. Spreitzer, and Edward E. Lawler III, eds. *The Leader's Change Handbook: An Essential Guide to Setting Direction and Taking Action.* San Francisco: Jossey-Bass, 1998.

Copley, Frank B. *Frederick W. Taylor: Father of Scientific Management, Vol. 1.* New York: Kelley, 1969.

Cordeiro, Wayne. *Doing Church as a Team.* Honolulu: ICM Press at New Hope Christian Fellowship, 1998.

Davidson, James Dale, and Rees Mogg. *The Sovereign Individual: How to Survive and Thrive During the Collapse of the Welfare State.* New York: Simon & Schuster, 1997.

Davis, Stan, and Christopher Meyer. *Blur: The Speed of Change in the Connected Economy.* Reading, Mass.: Addison-Wesley, 1998.

Easum, William. *The Church Growth Handbook.* Nashville: Abingdon Press, 1990.

_____. *How to Reach Baby Boomers.* Nashville: Abingdon Press, 1991.

Fleming, David L. "Models of Spiritual Direction." *Review for the Religious* 34 (1974): 351-57.

Foster, Richard. *Celebration of Discipline: The Path to Spiritual Growth.* San Francisco: HarperSanFrancisco, 1988.

Foster, Richard J., and James Bryan Smith, eds. *Devotional Classics.* San Francisco: HarperSanFrancisco, 1993.

Frauenfelder, Mark. "The Holo Trinity." *Wired* (July 1998): 7.

Gleick, James. *Chaos: Making a New Science.* New York: Penguin Books, 1988.

Golman, Daniel. *Emotional Intelligence: Why It Can Matter More Than IQ.* New York: Bantam, 1997.

Greely, Andrew. *The Sociology of the Paranormal: A Reconnaissance.* Beverly Hills, Calif.: Sage Publications, 1975.

Greenleaf, Robert. *The Servant as Leader.* Indianapolis: The Greenleaf Center, 1970.

Handy, Charles. *The Age of Unreason.* Cambridge, Mass.: Harvard Business School, 1991.

Harman, Willis. *Global Mind Change.* San Francisco: Berrett-Koehler, 1998.

Heifetz, Ronald. "The Leader of the Future." *Fast Company* (June 1999): 132.

Helgesen, Sally. *Female Advantage: Women's Ways of Leadership.* New York: Doubleday, 1995.

Henderson, D. Michael. *John Wesley's Class Meeting: A Model for Making Disciples.* Nappanee, Ind.: Evangel Publishing House, 1997.

Hestenes, Roberta. *Turning Committees into Communities.* Colorado Springs: Navpress, 1991.

Hinson, Glen E. *The Early Church: Origins to the Dawn of the Middle Ages.* Nashville: Abingdon Press, 1996.

Huxley, Aldous. *Brave New World.* Madison, Wis.: Demco, 1969.

Ignatius. *The Spiritual Exercises of St. Ignatius.* Translated by Anthony Mottola. New York: Doubleday, 1964.

Irenaeus. *The Treatise of Irenaeus of Lugdunum Against the Heresies.* Translated and edited by F. R. Montgomery Hitchcock. London: Society for Promoting Christian Knowledge, 1916.

Jones, Laurie Beth. *The Path: Creating Your Mission Statement for Work and for Life.* New York: Hyperion, 1996.

Kanigel, Robert. *The One Best Way: Frederick Winslow Taylor and the Enigma of Efficiency.* New York: Viking Press, 1997.

Kelly, Kevin. *Out of Control: The New Biology of Machines, Social Systems, and the Economic World.* Reading, Mass.: Addison-Wesley, 1994.

_____. *New Rules for the New Economy.* New York: Viking Press, 1998.

Kelsey, Morton T. *Companions on the Inner Way: The Art of Spiritual Guidance.* New York: Crossroad Publishing, 1995.

Kempis, Thomas à. *The Imitation of Christ.* Translated by William C. Creasy. Notre Dame, Ind.: Ave Maria Press, 1989.

Kiefer, Charles, and Peter Senge. *Transforming Work.* Edited by John D. Adams. Alexandria, Va.: Miles River Press, 1998.

Kise, Jane. *LifeKeys: Discovering Who You Are, Why You Are Here, What You Do Best.* Minneapolis: Bethany House, 1996.

Kolb, David. *Experiental Learning.* Englewood Cliffs, N.J.: Prentice-Hall, 1984.

Kouzes, James M., and Barry Z. Posner. *Encouraging the Heart: A Leader's Guide to Rewarding and Recognizing Others.* San Francisco: Jossey-Bass, 1999.

Krefft, Jim. "Designing for the 21st Century." *Journal of Business Strategy* (November/December 1998).

Kuhn, T. S. *The Structure of Scientific Revolutions,* 2nd ed. Chicago: University of Chicago Press, 1970.

McGregor, Douglas, and Warren G. Bennis. *The Human Side of Enterprise.* New York: McGraw-Hill, 1985.

Malphurs, Aubrey. *Values Driven Leadership: Discovering and Developing Your Core Values for Ministry.* Grand Rapids: Baker Books, 1996.

Mazlish, Bruce. *The Fourth Discontinuity: The Co-evolution of Humans and Machines.* New Haven: Yale University Press, 1995.

Merton, Thomas. *Spiritual Direction and Meditation.* Collegeville, Minn.: The Liturgical Press, 1960.

Morgan, Gareth. *Images of Organization: The Executive Edition.* San Francisco: Berrett-Koehler, 1998.

Morris, Danny E. *Yearning to Know God's Will.* Grand Rapids: Zondervan, 1997.

Mumford, Lewis. *The Transformation of Man.* New York: Harper Bros., 1956.

Negroponte, Nicholas. *Being Digital.* New York: Random House, 1996.

Niebuhr, Richard. *Radical Monotheism and Western Culture.* Louisville: Westminster John Knox, 1993.

Overman, Dean. "Not a Chance." *American Enterprise* (September/October 1998): 34-47.

Pascarella, Perry. *The New Achievers.* Monroe, La.: Free Press, 1984.

Peterson, John L. "The Futurist." *Fast Company* (February/March 1998): 30.

Piaget, Jean. *Genetic Epistemology.* New York: Columbia University Press, 1970.

Picard, Rosalind W. *Affective Computing.* Cambridge, Mass.: MIT Press, 1997.

Polkinghorne, John C. *Belief in God in an Age of Science.* New Haven: Yale University Press, 1998.

Robinson, Alan G., and Sam Stern. *Corporate Creativity: How Innovation and Improvement Actually Happen.* San Francisco: Berrett-Koehler, 1997.

Senge, Peter. *The Fifth Discipline: The Art and Practice of the Learning Organization.* New York: Doubleday, 1994.

_____. *The Fifth Discipline Fieldbook.* New York: Doubleday, 1994.

Slaughter, Michael. *Spiritual Entrepreneurs: Six Principles for Risking Renewal.* Nashville: Abingdon Press, 1995.

Smith, Brad. "What's Next on the Horizon: Team Ministry in the 21st Century." *Next* 9 (February 1995).

Sparrow, G. Scott. *I Am with You Always: True Stories of Encounters with Jesus.* New York: Bantam, 1995.

Stoll, Cifford. *Silicon Snake Oil: Second Thoughts on the Information Highway.* New York: Doubleday, 1996.

Sweet, Leonard. *AquaChurch.* Loveland, Colo.: Group Publishing, 1999.

_____. *SoulTsunami.* Grand Rapids: Zondervan, 1999.

Tapscott, Don. *Growing Up Digital: The Rise of the Net Generation.* New York: McGraw-Hill, 1997.

Tippler, Frank. *The Anthropic Cosmological Principle.* Oxford: Oxford Press, 1990.

Tulgan, Bruce. *The Pocket Manager's Guide to Generation X.* Amherst, Mass.: HRD Press, 1997.

Waldrop, M. Mitchell. *Complexity: The Emerging Science at the Edge of Order and Chaos.* New York: Touchstone Books, 1993.

Warren, Rick. *The Purpose Driven Church.* Grand Rapids: Zondervan, 1996.

Wheatly, Margaret J. *Leadership and the New Science: Learning About Leadership from an Orderly Universe.* San Francisco: Berrett-Koehler, 1999.

Wheatly, Margaret J., and Myron Kellner-Rogers. *A Simpler Way.* San Francisco: Berrett-Koehler, 1999.

White, Randall P., Phil Hodgson, and Stuart Crainer. *The Future of Leadership: Riding the Corporate Rapids into the 21st Century.* London: Pitman Medical, 1996.

Wilber, Ken. *The Marriage of Sense and Soul: Integrating Science and Religion.* New York: Broadway, 1998.

Wills, Dick. *Waking to God's Dream: Spiritual Leadership and Church Renewal.* Nashville: Abingdon Press, 1999.

About the Cover

I HAVE BEEN A FAN OF SCIENCE-FICTION FILMS AND television ever since I was a very young boy. The idea of the wormhole is one that I have been very familiar with for quite some time. When my partner in ministry, Len Wilson, e-mailed to tell me that Bill Easum wanted our assistance on the cover for this book, I was very excited. The challenge of breathing visual life into this somewhat abstract concept was one I found both difficult and rewarding.

I love Bill's use of a wormhole as a metaphor for change. For three years I served as a member of the Ginghamsburg United Methodist Church worship design team and on its media staff. It was there that I learned the effectiveness of using metaphor to bring a deeper level of retention and understanding to ideas expressed by a speaker and/or author. In a short e-mail conversation with Bill Easum about this metaphor and cover, I began to understand for myself the ideas he would be expressing.

It was my hope to emulate photos I'd seen, both real and imagined, from Sci-Fi shows like *Star Trek: Deep Space Nine.* The majority of my time on this image was spent creating the wormhole itself. The wormhole, along with the stars and space around it were digitally painted from scratch. The Earth was also created digitally, using a 3-D animation program. The Earth texture that was wrapped around a 3-D sphere was obtained from NASA's website. Text was then placed over the image using fonts that compliment the "space feel" of this piece.

It is my hope that through this cover I have given you a deeper understanding of what *Leadership On The Otherside* is all about.

Digital Artist,
Jason Moore
jmoore@lumicon.org
www.lumicon.org